Business Solutions for Budget Managers in Health and Personal Social Services

W J Bryans FCIS, FHSM

LONGMAN

Business Solutions for Budget Managers in Health and Personal Social Services

Published by Longman Information & Reference
Longman Group Limited, Westgate House, The High, Harlow,
Essex CM20 1YR, United Kingdom.

Telephone: (01279) 442601
Facsimile: (01279) 444501

First Published 1994

A catalogue record for this book is available from the British Library.

ISBN 0-582-25532-5

Printed in Great Britain by BPC Wheatons Ltd, Exeter

This book is dedicated to my wife, Edith, without whose support it could never have been written.

How to get the best from this book

Objectives

- Budget managers can improve the quality of their services through better financial performance.
- Even in a climate of fierce competition for market shares and resources it is possible to create a surplus for service development by:
  - strategic management of external and internal financial environments;
  - operational management of workloads and resources; and
  - tactical intervention to limit budget fluctuations to tolerable levels.
- Managers can develop a budget management process that provides them with a framework in which they successfully evaluate, implement and intervene.
- There is a variety of devices that facilitate that process.
- At appropriate times, selected techniques can be applied so that the desired result is achieved. This means that managers must be competent in dealing with the prevalent culture and be amenable to altered priorities.
- These competences need to endow managers with sensitivity to the organisational and management development requirements. They must provide an adequate mechanism to harmonise objectives.
- This book will help managers accomplish these complex tasks.
- *Business Solutions for Budget Managers* is a definitive statement of business principles as they should be applied to budget management in the modern health and social services business environment.
- After reading this book, first-time and prospective budget managers will be equipped to tackle budget problems in a systematic and purposeful way, which can be tested against their budget performance so that improved competence is demonstrated.
- It will be useful to managers in all disciplines, including social services, who endeavour to improve their own performance and the performance of their services. It will also be of interest to all those who work in or with other public, private and voluntary sector organisations.
- It should also form part of that body of management literature which is the core of academic reading.

Content

The advent of the internal market places a predominating need to obtain contracts.

Many other current business initiatives put an emphasis on financial performance. Influences such as competitive tendering, market testing, competing for quality, expenditure survey outcomes, etc, affect the overall financial climate.

The financial climate, which often resembles a near-0 growth, has an impact on purchasing, providing and resource budget capacity in health and personal social services.

Alteration in the balance of care and community care initiatives has generated a range of dependency-related problems. These are now widely perceived to require a carefully integrated organisation and management approach that clearly puts the patient or client first.

The promotion of the work-place as a management college is the basis that is used to enhance organisational compatibility and management competence.

The book bridges the gaps that exist between budget, business and contracting for care management. It emphasises the inextricable links between organisational and individual management performance.

Each of the 12 chapters includes a list of objectives and describes the theory and practice applicable to the topic, with appropriate illustrations, examples and a case study.

Structure

The book is divided into three parts:

1. *Strategic management of the financial environment* — individual manager's requirements to survive in the internal and external environment with particular emphasis upon the prevalent business culture and its effect on the direction of expenditure.
2. *Operational management and tactical intervention* — organisation, structure, and business methodology applicable to the management of workload and resources in the contractual situation is the main theme of this part. Intervention is examined in the context of the key tasks in financial management (planning, profiling monitoring, intervening and monitoring), and in the context of the alteration in the balance of care.
3. *Performance* — Criteria favoured by the organisation and which influence the financial climate are dealt with in this part. There is emphasis on performance measurement, and the improvement of performance. The acquisition and abuse of goodwill also features.

These matters are the basic principles which will be further developed in the following chapters. The structure is:

PART 1 PART 2 PART 3

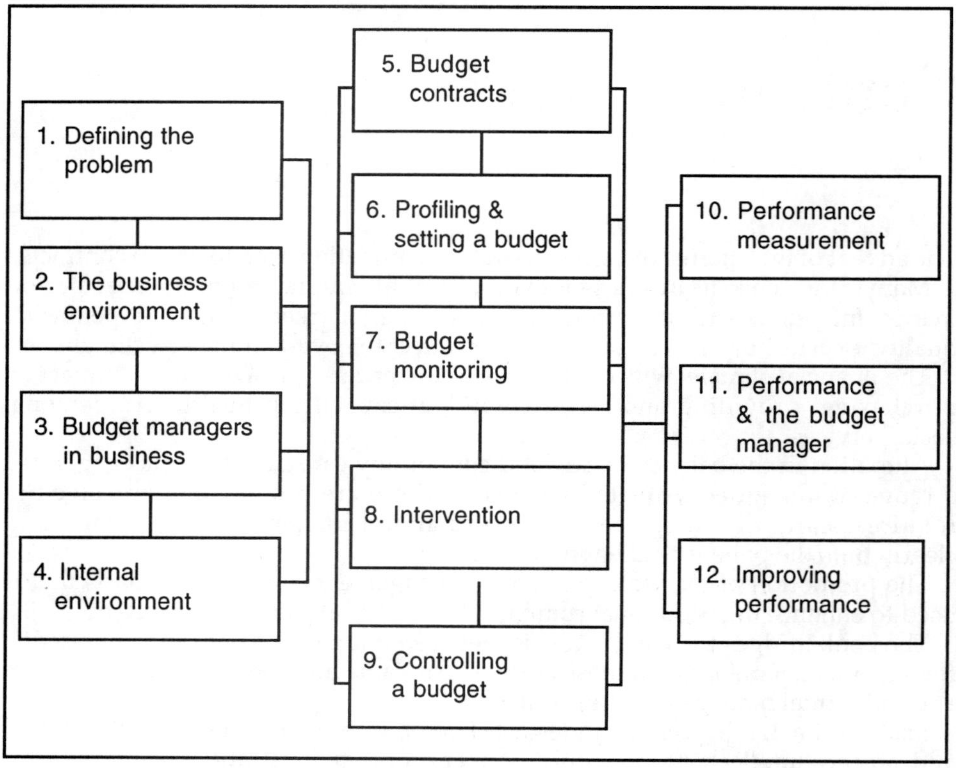

Contents

1

Defining the problem(s)

Objectives

The objectives of this chapter are to examine the main issues and in general terms set out the various problems which confront modern budget managers. Budget problems are usually first manifested in budget reports, but the underlying causes are complex. This is mainly the result of the reform programme.

Appropriate solutions are dependent on the correct diagnosis of the problem, or problems. In this chapter these problems are connected to the business culture topics:

- The main business elements that regulate financial management are identified.
- The need for an integrated approach is discussed.
- The outline effect of the budget manager's market share on income and budget is shown.
- The relationship between cost, case load and budget is defined.
- The impact of case mixtures and an alteration in care balance on resource consumption through increased dependency is demonstrated.
- The contract capability and criteria for the measurement of income are identified.
- Examples of significant variations and the need for *planned* intervention is emphasised.

The chapter continues with:

- An analysis of the main problems.
- A summary of their causes.
- An outline of various business solutions.
- A competence based approach to budget security.

Arising from this, the overall structure of the book is established.

Familiar territory

In every age where money has been the currency of business, budget managers have experienced the basic problem that they have too little. Inevitably their problems have been compounded by their masters requiring too much. Where a financial plan produces a surplus, demands upon savings always outstrip the reality. If there is a deficit, then the manager is automatically to blame. In the unlikely case of a balance being achieved there is usually an inference that the performance was still somehow disappointing.

The last decade has seen the growth of a business culture in health and social services management. Coterminous with this has been a subtle shift away from the concept of **budget *holding*** and towards an emphasis upon **budget *management*.** In many ways this change can be viewed as a move from simpler passive control of a budget to the much more complex active intervention in order to compete.

In comparison with their predecessors, who enjoyed the benefit of a fairly consistent financial growth rate, modern budget managers are confronted with more complex tasks. A near-0 financial growth rate, together with requirements to alter the balance of care consistent with the mixed economy, results in significant budget problems.

Whatever the era, budget problems continue to depress budget managers. Overspendings seem to dominate and can, if allowed, become an obsession at all levels. This does not have to be so.

Budget management problems are usually first detected in the financial reporting mechanism. For most budget managers the pattern shown in Table 1.1 will be familiar.

Care group	Budget for Month 5 £k	Spend for Month 5 £k	Over spend £k	Under spend £k
Community workers	50	60	10	
Residential contracts	30	25		5
Housing partnership	15	21	6	
Community workers	25	20		5
Home helps	10	14	4	
Totals	130	140	20	10

Table 1.1

Familiar questions that arise are:

1. **Is it a true position?**
2. **Are the overspendings uncharacteristic?**
3. **Are there any seasonal fluctuations to be accounted for?**

Table 1.1 is, in respect of a budget, intended to cover the provision of services to mentally handicapped people. It has been subjected to an alteration in the balance of care in favour of the community. The origin of significant problems is to be found elsewhere in the system. This suggests an outline action plan from which a structured intervention may be developed (see Figure 1.1).

Plan	Preparation	Action
Secure internal information base		
• Check context of budget statement	• Look for historical pattern in spending levels (is variation seasonal, for example?)	• Assemble all relevant facts
• Determine significance of variation	• See guidance on toleration levels below	• Calculate toleration level
• Establish spending direction	• Look for development or or retraction rate	• Test against business criteria
• Make minor changes to commitments	• Decide if necessary and appropriate	• Apply marginal adjustments
External		
• Examine income parameters: –quality –market share –price	If the above internal steps are inadequate, the contract conditions need to be re-evaluated and possibly renegotiated	• Test whether income is properly translated into budget data • Test expected income levels
Internal		
Look for additional capacity in resource budgets—particularly in the estate	This is a major piece of work and is dealt with in detail in Part 2 of the book	Rationalise any obvious spare or vacant resources

Figure 1.1. Outline action plan

The budget manager must see whether tactical intervention is the best solution in this case or whether it is necessary to go further. The manager also needs to know if underspendings can be used or whether they are only temporary.

Significant variations

When we look at this position in terms of the year's performance to date, it is evident that there is a consistent over-commitment in the case of hospital, housing association partnerships, and the home help budgets (see Table 1.2). However, contracts with private providers and expenditure in the community have balances remaining.

Care group	Budget for year	Spend to month 4	Spend @ month 5	Cumulative spend to 5	Remainder
	£k	£k	£k	£k	£k
Hospitals	750	240	60	300	450
Residential Contracts	350	95	25	120	230
Housing partnership	180	84	21	105	75
Community workers	300	76	20	96	204
Home helps	100	52	14	66	34
Totals	1,680	547	140	687	993

Does not agree with statement*

Substantial over commitment

Remainders indicate that programmes are not fully operational

Continuation of resource consumption rate means (cumulative spend divided by number of months X months remaining). **687/5x7=961.8** This would result in an underspending of **£31.2k** in the year and this contradicts the report

* The calculation reveals a contradictory position to that reported in the Month 5 statement. The budget manager has to get a clearer picture of the overall situation before intervention can be undertaken. Relationships that exist between various business elements need to be clarified.

Table 1.2. Identifying budget variations

> **The budget manager must look at the business plan before any dramatic revision—*especially the implementation of additional spending plans*—takes place.**

- In the case shown in Tables 1.2 and 1.3, the business plan reveals that the hospital portion refers to a high dependency provision for which retraction is not yet complete.
- The budget of £750k for the year includes a core element of £600k for the profoundly handicapped and it is the pro rata portion of this that is shown as the budget for month 5 [£50k].
- The rest (£150k) is held in reserve pending the completion of already vacated accommodation which is to be used for respite and day care.
- It was originally intended that this would be competed in time for use during the last three months of the financial year (Jan–Mar). On the other hand investment in the community aspects have not been fully realised.

A revised budget statement for Month 5 would need to be provided so that the whole picture is clearer (see Table 1.3).

Care group	£k	Budget for year £k	Budget for Month 5 £k
Hospital (continuing care)		600	50
reserves – respite care	100		
– day care	50	150	–
Residential contracts		350	30
Housing partnership		180	15
Community workers		300	25
Home helps		100	10
TOTALS		1680	130

Table 1.3 Revised budget statement for Month 5

Managers need to be keenly aware of the consequences in resource terms and they must articulate them at the proper time. That is to say, when the business plan that will regulate the contract process is being developed. They need to be competent.

A budget manager, 'X', had five subgroups. Four were overspent. One had a modest underspending. 'X' decided to take up the single underspending with the result that every one of the subgroups was overspent.

The benefit of an integrated approach

These problems are seated in the balance that managers have to strike between the retraction in one part of service delivery and development in another. In consequence, some managers may be net losers, some net gainers and some may in financial terms maintain an equilibrium. The emerging financial pattern is therefore much more fluid. Its management is centred upon careful organisation of a growth rate which nears zero.

The modern budget manager has therefore to deal with a significantly wider range of issues. In addition to skills which render a healthy budget balance, they must acquire business intelligence and business acumen. These will help them survive in an essentially competitive market place.

A wider range of causes also provides greater opportunities for astute managers to enhance their financial position, *but* they must be equipped

In order to secure maximum financial advantage, budget managers need to demonstrate an *active* as opposed to a *passive* budget management approach. It is vital that any action taken is properly studied and informed. Managers need to develop a capacity for adopting an evaluating process which enables them to moderate their intervention with a more mature business sense. It is no longer possible to isolate the budget as an independent element in the management process.

The budget management process needs a more holistic approach. It has to include consideration of market place and contractual demands. Sound budget management must therefore be based upon a series of responses which are dependent on methods that integrate various elements.

Budget managers need to be sensitive to market demands. They must be prepared to supply at the right terms. *Quality, cost* and *price* are key considerations for competent contractors.

In the contracting situation, budget managers depend upon the income generated. Their market share, won either on their own initiative or as part of a corporate endeavour, is the dominating influence on case-load volumes and income. The translation of this into resources is controlled by the business planning mechanism, which will focus on the quality and balance of care being offered at a particular price level. This process is illustrated in Figure 1.2.

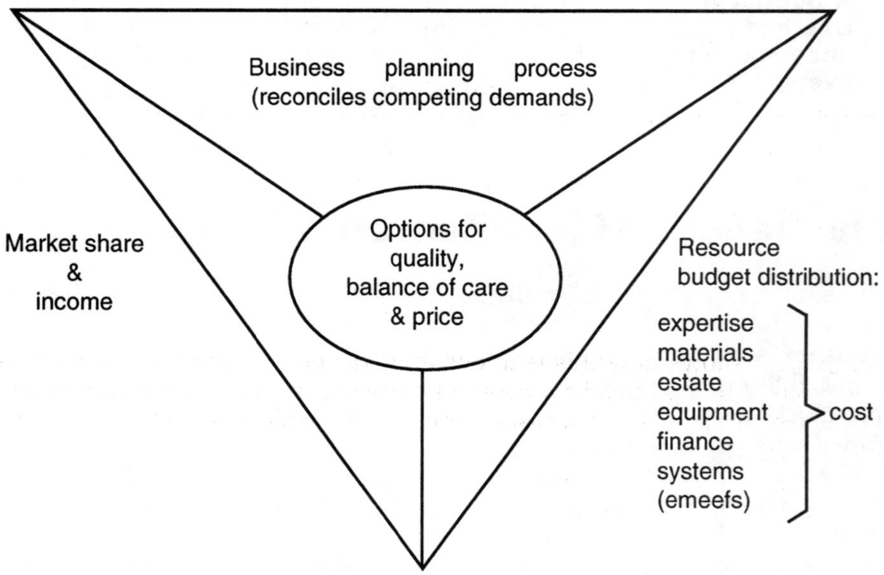

Figure 1.2. Integrated budget management process

Market shares

In a useful chapter on information technology in health care, the phenomenon that regulates the relationship between purchaser and provider is explained[1]. In extreme cases, where monopsony or monopoly are prevalent, the market tends to be dominated by one party or the other. Thus, where there is only one purchaser, provider units are in a less advantageous position. On the other hand, where there is nearly only one provider, for example the provision of regional specialties, the provider will have the advantage.

Purchasers want to maximise their purchasing power through competition. Providers want to maximise their market position by eliminating competition.

Assuming that it is a realistic option, the preference for purchasers and providers would seem to be contradictory. Purchasers would prefer to deal with the competition achieved where there are many providers. Providers, on the other hand, may have an advantage where there are many purchasers. In certain circumstances financial advantages are exploited through amalgamation or consortia arrangements. Where the market share is altered in this way, choice and accessibility criteria tend to be diminished.

To be effective as contractors, budget managers need to know how their particular market works.

Markets are seldom homogeneous in nature, nor can their size and scope be limited by artificial boundaries. It is, however, possible to obtain a feeling for the way in which markets operate by ignoring these complications and assuming that there was equality. Although this is a greatly simplified case, it is possible to calculate where market equalibrium exists. If the total busines available in a particular market place is (T), this is equal to the total number of shares (N) multiplied by the size of each share (S):

$$T = NS$$

Figure 1.3 shows how this relationship is developed and the equation can be subsequently refined to take account of particular circumstances. In this case, for a variety of reasons the purchaser might, for example, decide to contract for the core of business on the basis of working with around five main contractors. This means that the value of contracts let would be in the region of £60m each on average. The number of main providers would therefore be in the order of five. It would not therefore follow that they were all of equal size but it would make sense to ensure that there was a degree of uniformity, otherwise the number of contracts could not be managed and they would eventually be uneconomic.

Some contractors would therefore be specialists, for example the provision of acute services, or where the unit was big enough—a specialist group within this description, for example children's services. At the other end of the spectrum it might make economic sense to deal with a composite unit providing both hospital and community services.

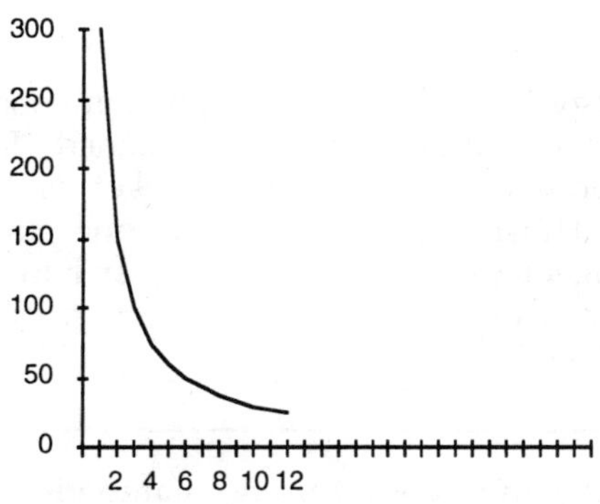

Figure 1.3. Internal market value = £300m

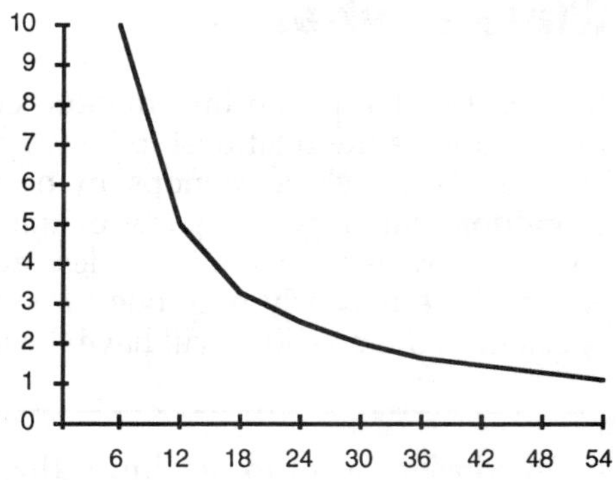

Figure 1.4. Market share = £60m

The same formula applies to the number and size of budgets within a budget system. This is illustrated in Figure 1.4. The difference here is the fact that there will only be one 'purchaser'—the host organisation. This characteristic has a direct bearing on budget management performance and is dealt with in detail in a later chapter.

Budget managers, whatever their business, location, or function *purchase* resources to enable them to *provide* the service required. They are both purchasers and providers.

Whether a budget is located in a provider or a purchaser organisation, budget managers within the confines of their domain are purchasers of adequate resource levels, **but to their external environment they are always in the role of service provider** (see Figure 1.5).

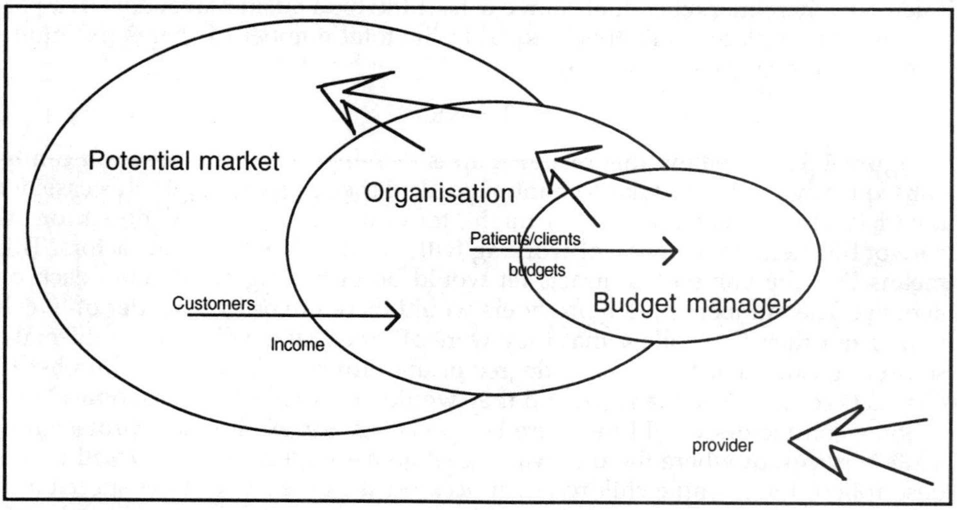

Figure 1.5. Simplifying relationships

Broadly, the relationship which exists between the potential market, the supplying organisation and the budget manager, is illustrated in Figure 1.5. The organisation's intrusion into the potential market place is regulated on a formal or informal basis through contract mediation. Similarly, the budget manager's internal domain is coterminous with budget boundaries and these are significantly influenced by the budget size. Thus, although the processes are essentially the same, customers become patients or clients and income becomes the budget. In this sense, variations either in volume terms or in terms of finance are variations to the contract and they must all be treated in that light.

Budget managers must make themselves totally aware of both the external and internal environments in which they intend to operate.

Customers and case loads

It is the combination of customer volume and the price mechanism which produces income. The price mechanism alone is not, however, the sole arbiter. Indeed, it might be argued that it is the quality product at the right price which is the dominant consideration. The 'right' price is not therefore the cheapest price and it is mainly achieved through the application of quality assurance and quality accreditation. Usually this is done by means of the Kings Fund Organisational Audit or similar device.

Competent contractors are successful if they can guarantee the five 'Rs'. They convince purchasers that they can supply—at the right *quality*, at the right *quantity*, at the right *price*, at the right *time*, at the right *place*.

Likewise, patient and client volumes convey a funding level to the budget manager. The relationship between volume and resource consumption is complicated by the degree of dependence exhibited. Many of the attributes which characterise the problems inherent in modern budget management are connected in some way with this equation. In Figure 1.6 the classical connection between cost workload and budget is illustrated.

Sometimes managers are inclined to ignore this relationship and seek savings from existing budget agreements. Where a specification is part of a contract this must be changed in order to comply with revised funding. This does not mean that managers should cease their pursuit of more cost effective ways of working.

A catering contractor was able to claim £80k pa savings on payroll by preparing breakfast at ward level using microwave techniques. This revised traditional methods of preparation and distribution using a central kitchen. Here there was broad compliance with the specification but the way of working was different.

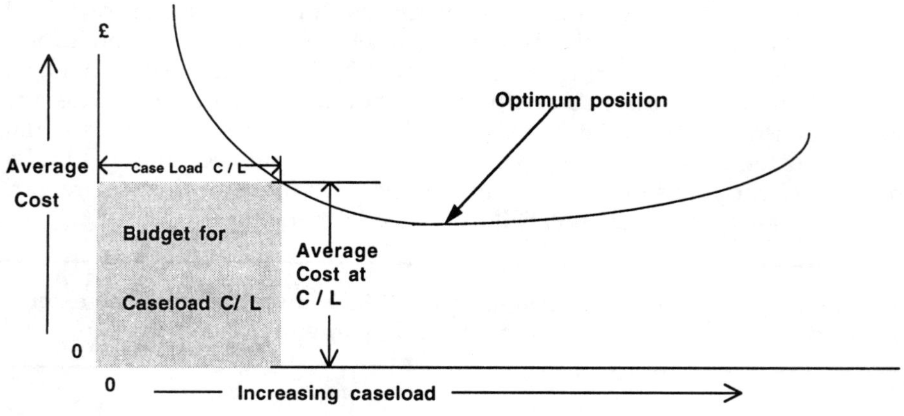

- The average cost is calculated for a series of caseload values by referring to the specification for quality and resource inputs.
- As caseload increases, average cost falls until the optimum point is reached.
- At any particular point, for example where the caseload is C/L, the budget must be calculated by multiplying the average cost at that point by the caseload.

Figure 1.6. Average cost/caseload/budget relationship

Case mixtures and alteration in balance

An alteration in the balance of care in favour of a more appropriate form of care means shorter stays at any stage but there is a concentration on higher dependency levels. In Figure 1.7 the new budget is shown for a shorter stay but an increased dependency level. In certain cases it is easy to see how this might actually be a more expensive option.

The main reason for this is the increased proportion of fixed charges which a budget manager must bear. In other words, there is a further shift away from the optimum position. In order to survive in these circumstances the budget manager would have to obtain a greater market share and/or rationalise beds/places etc.

Where case mixes are more complex than the situation in Figure 1.7 a separate budget calculation would be neccessary for each one—if the detail could be identified. There would, nevertheless, have to be a number of assumptions relating to the apportionment of fixed and other costs. This process becomes more and more difficult as the system is refined and there is a danger that sight may be lost of the main objectives. This aspect is a major problem for providers who wish to move away from volume costs and towards a more sophisticated procedure-based contractual arrangement.

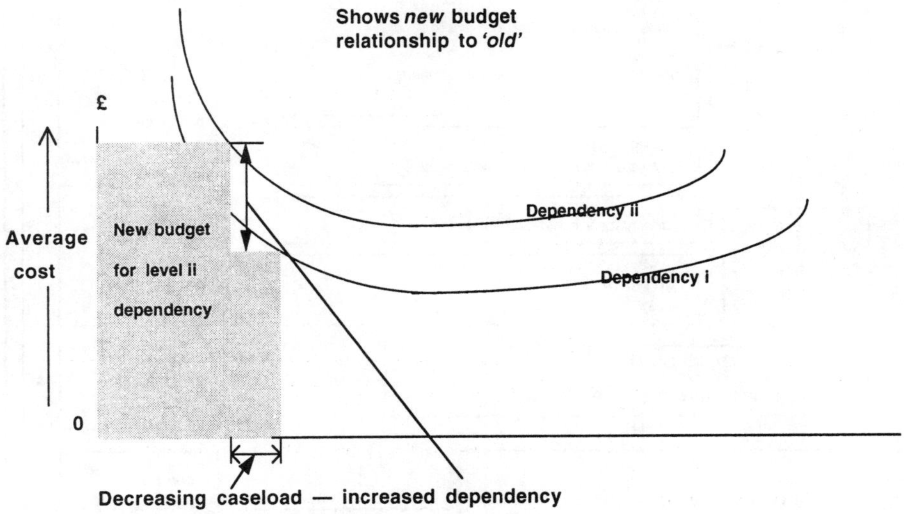

The figure shows how a reduction in caseload, coupled with an increased dependency level, must be reflected in a recalculation of the budget which may be actually larger than the old budget.

Figure 1.7. Alteration in the balance of care

Organisational compatibility in competence development

Distinction here must be made when defining competence and compatibility. They can be mutually exclusive, and the development of both competence and compatibility is an organisational problem which entails the translation of settlements from the spirit and intention of the negotiation process to the workplace.

In assessing a position, senior managers are confronted with a wide choice spectrum of management development options whose application would doubtless benefit the individual or group. Selection is inevitably constrained by the shortage of facilitating resources. In addition, managers often experience difficulty in deciding upon developmental priorities. As a first step it is worthwhile establishing acceptability criteria which will help identify the context and condition, and provide an outline profile. This process is shown in Figure 1.8.

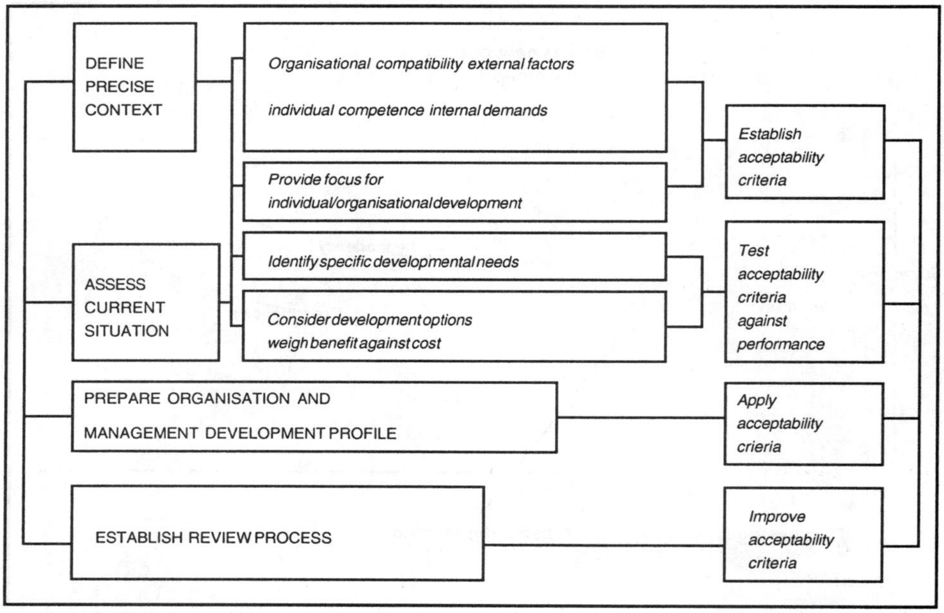

Figure 1.8. Process of acceptability criteria

Solutions

The solutions demonstrated in this book relate to budget management in a mixed economy of care. They are to be interpreted in the specific context and environment and must be underpinned by a measured investment of time and effort in the development of the organisation and the manager. The main points which will be developed are:

- **Need for an integrated approach** to budget management problems.
- **Near-0** financial growth climate impact on purchasing, providing and resource budget capacity in health and personal social services.
- **Clarity** in determining quality and its value.
- **Financial and business interface** between care in the community and longer-term, acute, and other forms of care.
- **Evaluation of options** and their application to development and retraction models.
- **Competence**-based approach to budget management development.
- **Focus** upon the effect that cost of resources have on price space and time as significant limiting factors.
- **Contemporary** management techniques, such as the use of option appraisals.
- **Resource mobility management** as an enabling device.
- **Commitment management** as a potent budget management tool.

Budget managers need to acquire the skills and insight to enable them to apply the correct form of intervention at the most appropriate time...

- **Know your business capacity.**
- **Know your environment.**
- **Know your budget capability.**
- **Know how to improve your performance.**

Key points summary

- Improving financial performance is complex but need not be depressing.
- Financial performance is affected by both internal and external factors.
- Quality and price are key to successful contracting.
- Budget managers in whatever function or location are providers.
- Budget statements and associated information are evidence of the budget manager's contract conditions.
- For patient and client services, falling inpatient and residential client numbers result in increased dependency. Compensation for this tendency must be translated into a rationalisation of resources.
- For hotel and support services budget managers there is commensurate pressure upon budget structures.
- Increased numbers and increased dependency in community care must be subjected to business considerations.
- There is no room for doubt about the precise interpretation of the over and underspending positions.
- Potential for reduced funding as a result of possibly better care options needs to be carefully evaluated.
- Management must be clear about the relationships connecting quality, pricing and resourcing.
- Preparation for more aggressive competition is essential.
- Development of management potential must be carefully considered.

Case study

- Hopefields Disability Resource Centre provides comprehensive programmes to a wide range of client groups. It opens Monday–Friday, from 9.00 am to 4.30 pm. The centre also closes for two weeks in the summer, one week at Christmas and is closed during statutory holidays.
- At the end of the previous financial year there were 5,000 attendances at a cost of £100k. There has, however, been consistent audit criticism that the centre is not fully utilised.
- Hopefields is located in accessible premises convenient to the centre of a large town from which most of the clientele originate.
- As a result of the community reforms there is an increasing demand for an extension of services.
- Management carried out a review, and with the support of specialist voluntary workers it was possible to facilitate a further 1,000 attendences per year at an increased cost of £3k.
- Other options were examined:
  - extension of the catchment area by improving the transport service;
  - providing respite in the evenings to allow carers the chance to go out; and
  - opening on Saturday and Sunday to:
    - improve the overall scope of the facility;
    - absorb some of the demand; and
    - benefit from the economies of scale.

References

1. Bryans WJ (1994) Business Planning for Purchasers and Providers (D.1.4.2, *Information Management in Health Care*).

2

The business environment (know your environment)

Objectives

The objectives of this chapter are to:

- Explore in general terms various concepts relating to financial and business management.
- Examine issues concerned with managing the internal and external environments.
- Demonstrate the need for compatibility between business and budgetary management.
- Enlarge upon budget management principles and give an overview of the totality of the process.

Specifically the chapter covers:

- The major items on the management agenda.
- Business planning as an acceptable method of coping with competition in the internal market.
- How the process works to enhance the market share.
- The options for concentration on discrete areas of business activity.
- The effects which choices have on resources.
- Retraction and development models.
- Direction and scope of spending.
- Budget statements as a mode of communication.

The management agenda

The NHS and community reforms have presented managers with a formidable agenda. This differs significantly from the previous era when there was emphasis upon control of an apparently more stable situation. In budgetary and business terms this means that, while opportunities exist for better and more informed choices between diversification and specialisation, there are even greater constraints and risks imposed, partly by the market and partly by managers' ability to create mobility within their quota of already scarce resources.

There is no easy solution to these problems. Doubtless training and experience are important longer-term competences upon which successful managers will come to rely, but practising managers must react in their current state of readiness. They are almost daily confronted with a tide of initiatives, guidance, regulations, reports and commentaries. Frequently they are bound to respond to these almost by return.

Managers are concerned about the increasing lack of time at their disposal for the actual management task. This emphasises the need for strategic, operational and tactical competence.

Identification of key business issues affecting affordable care and treatment, and the demonstration of how the manager can best influence them, is essential.

In this context, the main items on the manager's agenda should be restricted to those matters that have a business significance. In other words, professional and other related considerations should be debated and agreed in other forums. Business aspects can then be woven into the overall strategy and given priority according to a protocol. Otherwise there will be confusion and delay in the execution of business and financial facets.

At the Budget Managers' Convention, 'X' claimed that against a background of increasing workloads and higher dependency spending was reduced in real terms. 'X' also claimed that there simply was not enough money in the budget.

Elements which might be considered as key are:

- Quality statements and measures.
- Alteration in the balance.
- Cost.
- Price mechanism.
- Marketing and contacting.
- Mobility and management of resources.

These elements react so that a change in one feature has an impact on one or more others.

Their relationships are more complex than might be expected. For example, an improvement in quality does not necessarily lead to an increase in cost or additional resource commitment, nor does a price increase necessarily mean that market share will be diminished. These apparently perverse characteristics are difficult to manage. This is why the government commends the use of techniques practised in industry and commerce as mechanisms to help managers cope with the disparate demands of the internal market. One such technique, now widely practised, is business planning.

Business planning

This is a process which leads managers through a series of steps so that they can clearly identify so-called 'discrete areas' of activity, which should be:

- developed and improved;
- maintained at present levels;
- activity reduced; or
- closed.

> **The Treasurer regretted 'X's outburst and said there were more appropriate forums for this kind of debate. Talking about how development monies must be found through better financial management, the treasurer was visibly surprised when this was not well received.**

- The application of business planning techniques is intended to liberate internal resources so that greater effectiveness results. Generally much of the business direction is initiated at national or regional level and in turn is reflected through the contracting arrangements.
- Thus, a provider will obtain a broad indication of expectation from management executive planning documents and from purchasing prospectuses. Similarly, purchasers are made aware of providers' intentions from their responses.
- Market trends, as expressed in referral patterns and other sources of market intelligence, will also have to be taken into account, Figure 2.1 illustrates how these features are interconnected.

Process characteristics

Essentially, the process facilitates the management of the internal and external environments. It also reconciles the requirements of the care regime with available resources.

The relationship between the internal and external environment is influenced by:

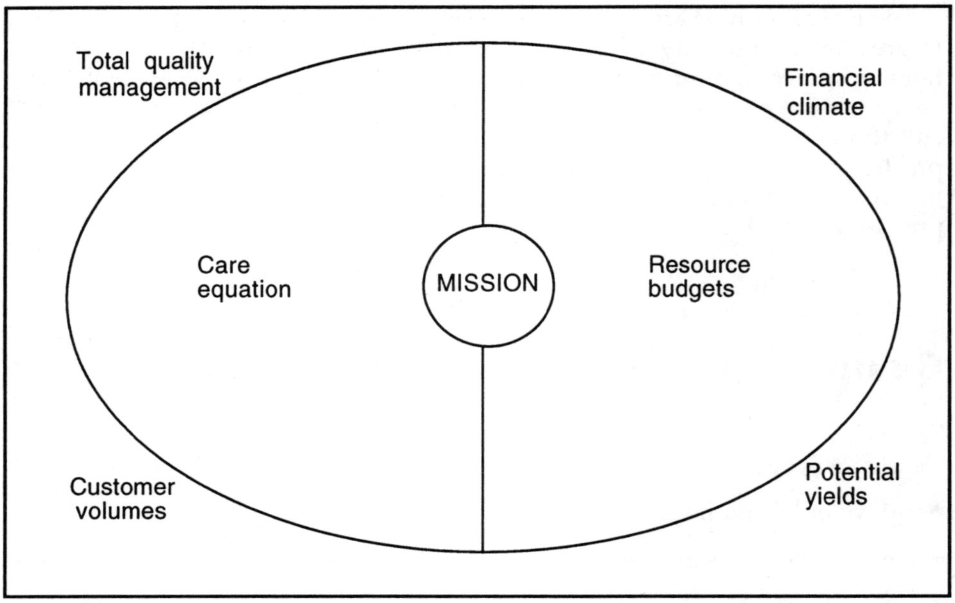

Figure 2.1. The planning process

- **Total quality management**—the commitment to quality standards, measures and improvements, which are known to beneficially influence the market share.
- **Customer volumes**— the numerical evidence of the market share is made amenable to analysis of referral and clinical or client management in order to conform with contract criteria.
- **Potential yields**— refers to the mechanism that links price and volume together to provide an income either as part of the contract or on an extra contractual basis. At another level, yield can also be attributed to quality outcomes in the benefit derived from a particular regime by the patient or the client.
- **Financial climate**— the mixture of political and economic pressures that must dominate all budget management considerations.

Together, these elements produce an envelope which contains the internal environment.

Instability in the model can be effectively utilised by astute managers to improve the operation of the internal environment. This is represented mainly by the interaction between the balance of care and the resource budgets necessary to support that care. The internal environment is clearly dependant on external factors but its careful management also contributes to the way these external factors behave. The characteristics are:

Care equation— is the balance that is struck between effectiveness and appropriateness. It is usually measured by the study of dependency levels in the categories of care provided. An alteration in the current status of the balance of care will have a profound effect on all the other factors.

Resource budgets — refers to the comprehensive budget mechanism that is used to manage all the resources within the system.

Where a climate of near-0 growth prevails, however, purchasing capacity is limited. The result is that development can occur only through either achieving a competitive edge or by concentrating upon discrete parts of the market. Usually a combination or mixture of both devices will be used. Some would argue that in many ways, these phenomena occur naturally. Whether this is so is a matter of debate. It is true, however, that where market pressures come to bear upon any organisation where there is multiple products there is a tendency towards specialisation and rationalisation. The areas that command the largest market shares are likely to be the focus for increase at the expense of smaller less viable parts. Figure 2.2 illustrates this.

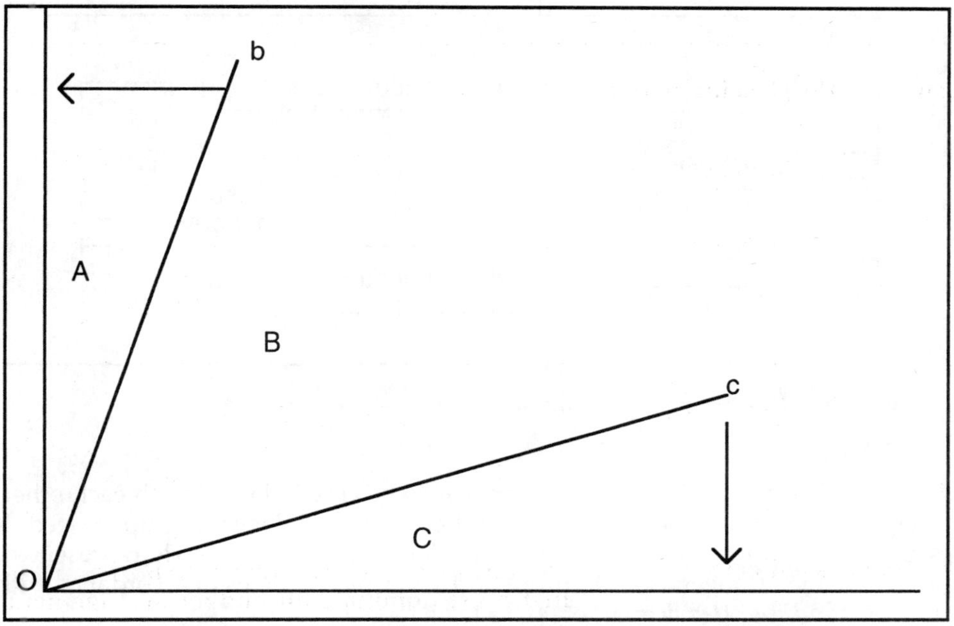

Figure 2.2. Market shares

As shown in the figure there is a tendency for sector B to grow at the expense of A and C, thus lines b and c tend to 0. In the near-0 growth climate the main pressure is on resource budgets to provide the capacity with which to rearrange service profiles. Participation and competence of the budget manager at all stages of the business planning and contractual management processes are therefore keys to success.

A robust business plan will evolve only when there is an adequate vehicle with which to carry it forward.

In order to capture the spirit of the corporate direction the complexity of this will have to be compatible with the scale of the operation. It is usual to reflect this in the type and number of teams. Thus, in an acute unit, business would be planned according to the range of clinical and other directorates. In a mixed unit providing a more seamless service team membership would be more diverse. It would be drawn from a range of hospital and community specialisms. This is not to give the impression that one is more difficult to manage than the other but, rather, that they are different. Figure 2.3 illustrates a general outline.

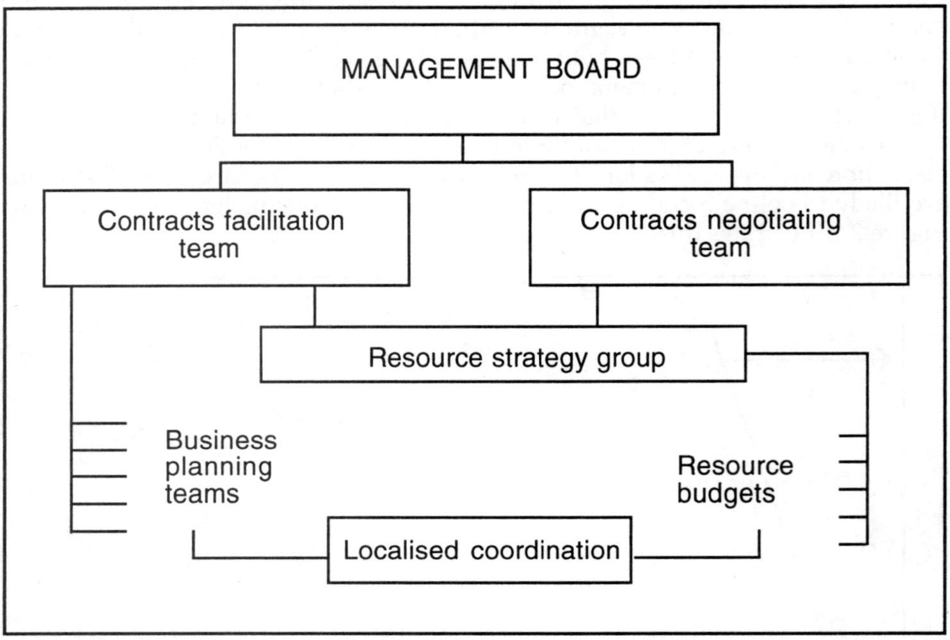

Figure 2.3. Outline business planning structure

Various functions are shown which appear to be closely linked with each other. These may be telescoped together or further expanded depending upon need. It is most important to ensure that all professional views are properly represented, otherwise the arrangement will be ineffective. A plan evolves in accordance with direction and the specific market that is to be targeted.

Discretion in business

This is achieved mainly by managing the external and internal environments. A catalogue of likely considerations is shown in Table 2.1.

Function	Current initiative	Development stage	Resource constraints
Quality	Charter compliance Process quality protocols Kings Fund OA process BS 5750 (trading services)	Additional funding Required Stage 3 Accreditation Stage 2	} Self funding
Health promotion	Comprensive programme Full screening programme	Continue review & coordination	} Additional staffing required
Child health	Increase immunisation % Address local issues Teenage pregnancy counselling Abuse counselling	10% increase Provide additional clinics & staff	} Increase in funding
Child & family care	Abuse & protection Reduce residential places Adoption & fostering Family resource centre	Roll out of professional training & policy on redeployment	Some savings from retraction but overall fund increase required
Mental handicap services	Reduce beds & places Respite & carer support Care management Housing partnership	Final stage of hospital & statutory reduction with care programmes	Implement policy-net retraction in all available resources
Community health care services	Paramedical services Night & respite Stimulate voluntary sector Enhance other local services	Implement community care reform programmes	Increase in resources necessary
Community social services	Care management Mixed economy of care	— " — — " —	
Services for the elderly	Reduce beds & places Contractural competence (with private sector) Coordinate community services	Alteration in the balance of care in favour of the community	Planned net savings from retraction in beds & places
Acute services	Increase turnover Reduce length of stay Streamline service profile Improve capability	Continuation of improvements in quality & efficiency	Retraction & redeployment of estate & staffing; review skill mix
Reserve fund	Plan to include provision for contingency reserve		

Table 2.1. Considerations for managing the external and internal environments

The thrust is clearly away from hospital and residential care towards a community-based market.

This is compatible with the reform initiatives. In marketing terms it is necessary to calculate 'how many @ how much?'. The results of which may produce a business plan like those in Tables 2.2 and 2.3.

Consequences:

- The business planning process must examine total activity.
- In terms of resource movement this is usually perceived as marginal.
- This is also the case where business volumes are concerned.

Developments	£ k	*Funding sources*	£k
Process quality [throughout unit]		Reduction in duplication Improved clinical accuracy Improved financial control	100
Health promotion Health promotion coordinator	30		NIL
Child health Improve immunisation take-up Increase enuretic clinic sessions Provide additional asthma clinic	50		NIL
Community heath care Increase twilight nursing Macmillan Partnership Home nursing Substance abuse counselling	70		NIL
Acute services Scanner appeal consequences Rehabilitation unit (RTAs) High dependency	150	Holiday closures Weekend closures Streamlining	300
Development reserve	100		
Totals	400		400

Table 2.2. Business plan example for a mixed acute and community unit summary

Developments		£k	*Funding sources*	£k
Care of the elderly Physiotherapy & OT services Home help developments Home laundry service Respite care improvements		100	Community care joint initiatives Hospital & residential places	100
Services for the physically and sensorily disabled				
Hospital rehabilitative unit—young PD	30			
Paramedic audit & assessment practice	10		Disabled Persons Act monies	
Specialist senior socialworker post	23		Hospital retraction	
Hopefields resource centre	7			
Resource centre for sensory impairment	12	82		82
Totals		182		182

Table 2.3. Business plan example for a social services joint venture with acute and community unit summary

Assuming that in Table 2.2, the two (volume and resources) share a parallel movement, there will be a significant alteration. This is illutrated in Figure 2.4.

The considerable movement which affects each service area must be addressed in two parts. However, this must be achieved in such a way as to secure the stability and continuity of the service being provided and at the same time obtaining the savings from the retraction to invest in proposed developments. In management terms such a demand is critical. It is so delicate that careful and steady

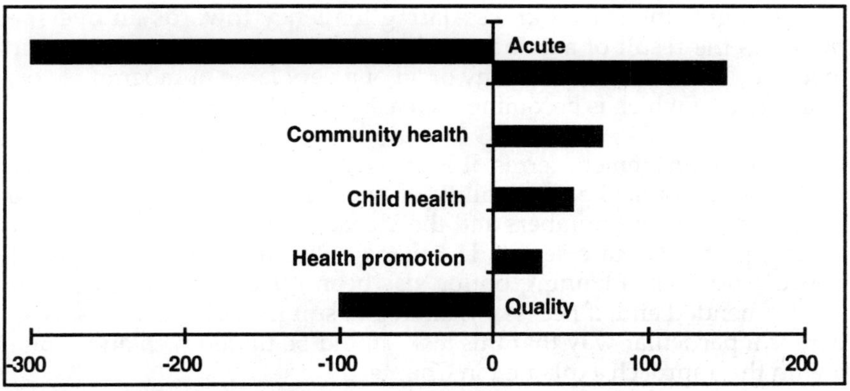

Figure 2.4. Retraction-development model

control of the process requires skill. It is also the single most potent factor in potential management failure.

This aspect is also a main characteristic that makes the post-reform era such a challenge to budget managers. Formerly managers appear only to have had the constant pressure of potential overspending to contend with. Now it seems that if other variables are introduced a seemingly impossible task has to be undertaken. At the same time this is the key to achievement.

> **While the task is made more complex, the important thing is to minimise delay in taking appropriate action to implement the plan.**

Inactivity is illustrated in Figure 2.5.

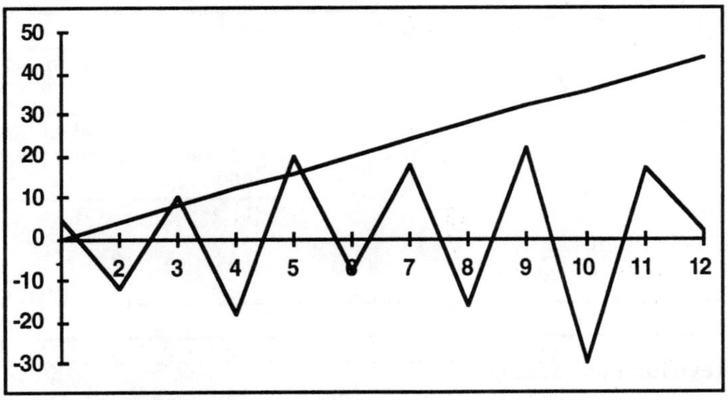

Figure 2.5. Performance comparison

The characteristic behaviour of a budget whose variation in or about the target line is indicated in the figure by the apparently haphazard movement of the lower graph.

- The manager is controlling over and underspendings in a resonably stable financial situation. It will therefore be a familiar picture to those experienced in conditions prevailing before the reforms.

- The straight line shows an escalating tendency towards an overspending which is the result of a manager's inability to control an emerging financial pattern. This may be due to any or all of a very large number of factors but it is a situation which is becoming increasingly well known.

In business management terms, it is frequently a financial manifestation of an inherent weakness in the availability of adequate resources, compounded by falling patient or client numbers and the increased dependency of those remaining in that particular care sector. The manager needs first to recognise the fact that once a business planning option has been selected it must be constantly updated, amended and, if necessary, altered to suit the circumstances.

There is a particular way that this task should be undertaken and it must conform with the approach explained in Chapter 1.

It involves:

- **Examining the market share.**
- **Examining resource budgets.**
- **Revising the plan.**

This process must be followed at all budget management stages. It is the key to understanding and managing the business environment (see Figure 2.6).

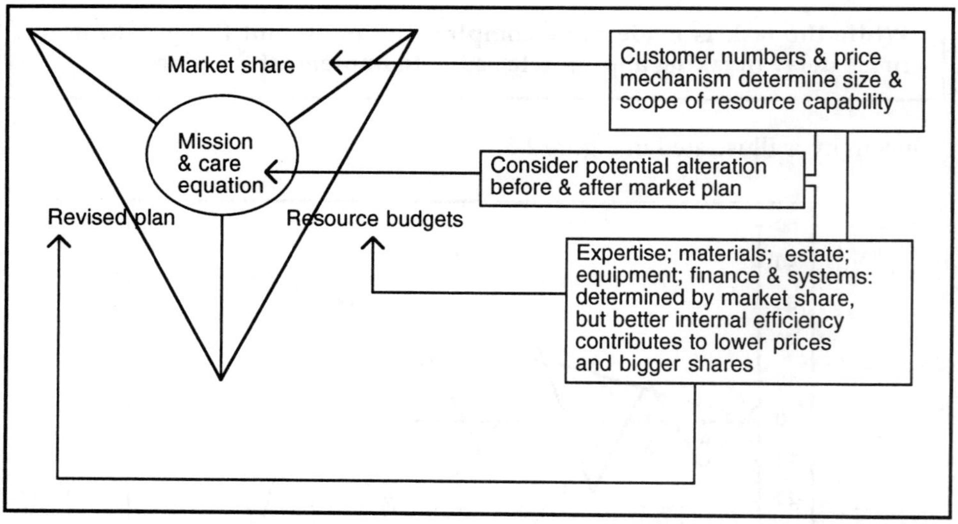

Figure 2.6. Revision methodology

Communication

In order to develop a management system communication media are essential. The assembly of facts and figures must both capture the initialisation and convey the need to take action. To make the media more effective, skills in managing within the budgetary environment must also be developed. Enhanced interpretative and intervention capacity is key to improved performance. Clarity, timing, focus, action and reaction are the objectives of good communication.

Table 2.4 sets out some points which must be considered.

Objective	Communication dependencies
Clarity	– Active participation in financial planning
	– Concentration upon fact
	– Familiarity with terminology
Timing	– Curtailing potential losses in transmission
	– Careful evaluation
	– Effective intervention
Focus	– Valuing income sources
	– Targeting significant variations
	– Improving performance
Action	– Compliance with financial plan
	– Creating enabling structure
	– Action planning
	– Communication audit
Reaction	– Diminishing turbulence
	– Containing hostility
	– Managing change

Table 2.4. The objectives of good communication

In general terms the level of communication within a particular public service is governed by a number of factors.

It is now possible to make a list of some of the main elements relating to budgetary management:

- The mechanism must clearly connect income with expenditure.
- It must work within the spending cycle (the financial year) so that accounting and budgetary information can be easily connected.
- The mechanism should make use of the control points characterised by the various events in the supply chain.
- Variations at each stage must be identified.
- There must be clear accountability.

Resource budget management

Budgetary management seems therefore to mean different things to different people and consequently there may be variations in different systems, attitudes and applications.

In citing an expenditure centre upon which a budget may be based there would be no obligation to go further and identify a budget holder who would have the authority for expenditure and the responsibility for the management of that particular budget. Yet, in order to obtain maximum advantage, it would seem reasonable that some delegation of spending authority would be an important facet of any system. Arising from this criterion, some form of report and dialogue would become necessary. This concept was never intended to indicate abdication but rather the recognition is generated at points which are usually remote from the location where the payment is made.

It is therefore frequently found that confusion exists as to both the interpretation and emphasis placed on the concept of budgetary management especially in the context of a control device. Many believe that budgetary management and budgetary control are one and the same thing. This is not so. Control is only a part of the management process. Confusion is also found to pervade the application of a system. It is necessary, therefore, to consider this idea of management against the background of feasibility. The objectives, financial or otherwise, have to be considered against the facilities with which a system is endowed in order to determine whether they are realistic.

The word 'management' is less than adequate in the precise sense, and evokes, for some, a delusion of completeness. This interpretation would suggest that budgetary capability is limitless. Extending the argument, with an emphasis upon the controlling aspect, expenditure curbs become objectives; the spending cycle is threatened; savings are demanded for their own sake. Although all these things are of course, possible, too much emphasis on this aspect may have a debilitating effect on goodwill and may in the long run be self defeating.

Everyone has their own ideas about interpretation, and, while some may see the main objective to be a reduction in expenditure, others may, in dramatic contrast, regard the budgetary management system as a spending incentive which is structured to eliminate waste. One is a crude instrument, the other a more sophisticated mechanism. Whatever the viewpoint, however, there is no doubt that both, with or without variations, can be effective. In a potentially changing financial climate, the perfectly controlled environment, even in the national context, can never be totally attained.

So it is, that in the extreme case, where budget managers appear to have maximum delegated authority and responsibility in that they may be given both purchasing power and the ability to negotiate contracts and pay, they can still be subject to inevitable environmental pressures which are outside their control. The reality is therefore that funding arrangements can never be wholly inflexible and must be subject to a degree of indulgence. Assessment of incremental credits either for inflationary purposes, for productive reasons, or as a tribute to original miscalculation, tend to embody the charisma of the more benign attitude.

For the sceptic, this evidence of failure will certainly be less than expectation.

Key points summary

- **Both business and budget management share the objectives common to the private citizen, the private sector, the public sector and the government.**
- **It is a continuous process of business and financial planning, intervention and control.**
- **The process ensures compatibility between the business and budget domains.**
- **It directs expenditure towards agreed business objectives.**
- **It ensures financial resources cover the cost of those objectives over a specified time.**
- **It keeps spending within the agreed pricing structure.**
- **It identifies areas where intervention may be necessary.**
- **Large-scale operations add further dimensions to the problems encountered by the individual.**
- **Budgetary management must be viewed as a *complete* approach to the achievement of business objectives. It encompasses:**
  - **the organisation and its objectives;**
  - **financial planning, monitoring, intervention and control within limits; and**
  - **the improvement and performance in a business culture.**
- **The major part of this activity is delegated to budget managers who are given authority to incur up to an agreed limit.**

Case study

Following continued criticism of management at Hopefields a feasibility study was carried out.

The main purpose of the study was to examine the various options which appeared to exist to see whether there was a genuine market to support extending the service. Costs were also calculated for each development.

The costs of likely service improvements were graded and sources of income identified. From this, it was possible to access a further £7k from disabled persons money.

This addition to the budget facilitated the extension of the transport service facilitating a further 1,000 attendences per annum.

3

Budget managers—competent contractors (know your business)

Objectives

The objective of this chapter is to examine the role of the budget manager as a contractor for service delivery. Budget managers need to be competitive but unless they have been directly exposed to the market economy, few really know how this can be measured or achieved. Budget managers can also use this information in their role as purchasers because the criteria are applicable to the exterior as well as the interior environments.

The chapter concentrates on lessons learned from competitive tendering and other initiatives. It shows how managers can subject their service to a critical examination as far as their competitiveness is concerned.

The chapter contains details on how:

- to take stock of present capacity and capability;
- to obtain evidence of competence;
- to prepare and comply with service specifications;
- a select list of competitive tenderers is prepared; and
- a contract is awarded and monitored.

The chapter also examines:

- Organisational characteristics,
- The way a budget should operate,
- Mutual expectations for improvements,
- Acceptable levels of delegated authority and responsibility.

Competitiveness

The emphasis on the business culture means that authorities, units and trusts have, to a greater or lesser extent, been exposed to a more competitive approach to the way business is transacted . In health, there is progress in achieving a better balance of care through shortening the length of time patients remain in hospital, resulting in fewer hospital beds and fewer hospitals. In social services, too, where there are fewer statutory homes for the elderly and for children, there is an emphasis on care management and the move towards a mixed economy of care. These initiatives are complemented by a growth in the private sector and improvements in community care.

Apart from these there would always have been a desire to limit spending to where it is most needed. In pursuit of this ambition, authorities constantly evaluate their financial position. In addition, the government also seeks to ensure that there is an equitable distribution of resources. To support this objective a formidable range of performance indicators have been developed which identify resource distribution per capita.

To survive in this environment budget managers need to take stock of their current position.

This process is illustrated in Figure 3.1.

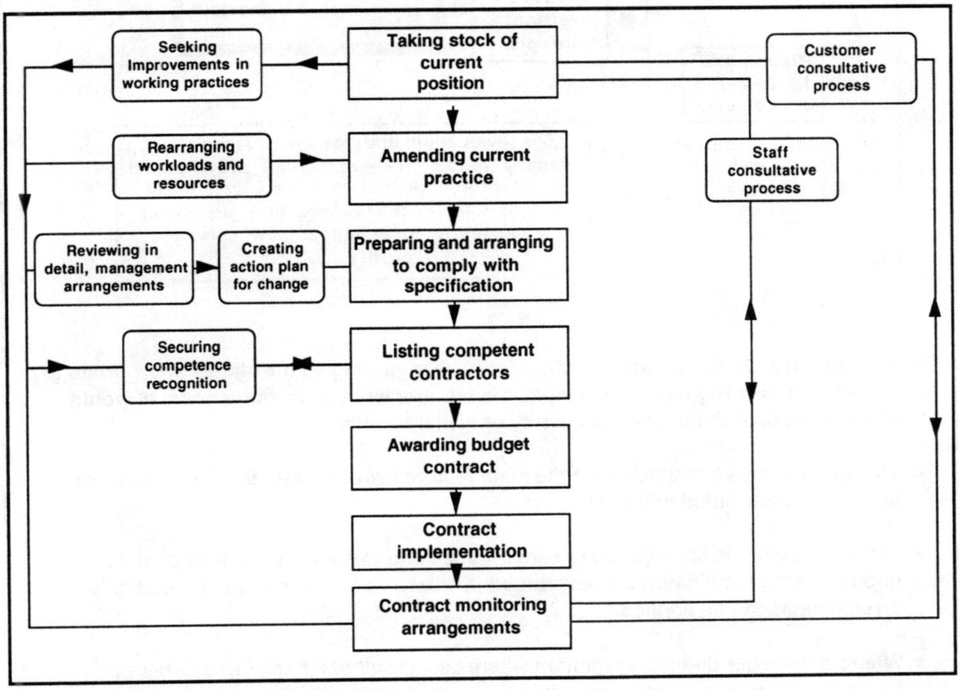

Figure 3.1. Testing competent contractors

The process is intended to be continuous and it should be made to fit in with the contracting year.

Taking stock

The main objective of the whole process is to enable budget managers to improve their contracting capacity and to involve them in an arrangement which will sustain them in a more competitive environment. In Figure 3.2 there is an outline of this process

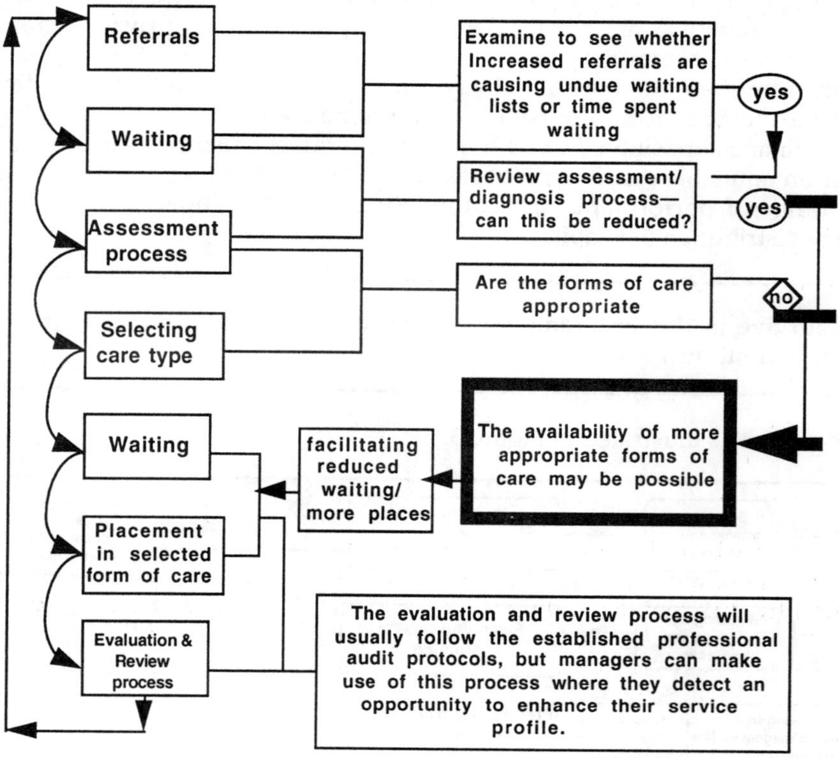

- **It is not possible to be completely prescriptive regarding all the stages appropriate to a particular care regime. For example, the requirements of an acute hospital would differ in detail to those of a community or social service.**
- **This outline does however cover the main features which affect the way resources have to be distributed and consumed.**
- **In that respect it is appropriate to care regimes and to support services such as supplies, payments payroll. In any situation where a service is requisitioned, this arrangement can be applied.**
- **Where a manager detects a situation where as a result of a back-log or where a surplus seems to have accrued, it is possible to move on to the next stage and redistribute the work-load in a more equitable fashion.**

Figure 3.2. Outline stock take of service provision

Taking stock highlights management areas where improvements made now will complement their attempts to comply later with specifications. This can later be used to reconcile care regimes with resource usage.

Amending current practice

Increasing quality, driving down costs.

The enabling factors behind this drive lie in the movement in patient and client work-loads. Where the regime is centred on fixed resources such as buildings, beds, places, etc, the use of these resources will be diminishing. In these cases, rather than continuing to invest in manpower for a diminishing return, managers must rationalise their services so that the best use is made of available resources.

It is important that where a significant change in current practice is contemplated, proper consultation takes place with both staff and customers. This consultation will be both formal and informal but if established and agreed practice is ignored the chance of effecting change is prejudiced.

Budget managers must work within and be committed to the philosophy, policies and procedures and structures which have been developed. Where there is perceived dissonance, the budget manager must seek to dispel or reduce these influences. Clearly this would differ from service to service. Budget managers must be clear of their role and the role of the organisation. Expectations would be significantly different depending upon the definition. For example, the expectations of a hospital consultant would be different from those of the head porter. Similarly the aspirations of the director of social services will differ in some respects to those of a home help.

Where there is to be change, therefore, costly disputes originating within and without the organisation have to be avoided. Budget managers therefore need to be clear about the organisation's policies. They need to consult with the relevant directors so that additional and unneccessary cost arising from dispute and delay is avoided.

A resident of some 15 years' standing in a home for the elderly successfully sought and obtained a judicial review of an authority's plans to close what was accepted to be her home.

The head porter was in dispute with the cleaning contractor over whose budget would bear the cost of mopping up the rain water in the front hall. The director of support services decided in favour of the contractor. Disgruntled, the head porter appealed to the general manager who eventually ruled that porters' duties included moping

Specification compliance

Detailed specifications are required to provide the basis of a sound contract. Purchasers generally draw up these specifications with the assistance and the eventual agreement of the provider. Budget managers may be consulted about the detail or they may, in certain circumstances, participate in the contracting process described in Chapter 2, either as a member of the contracts facilitating team or the negotiating team. In addition, each budget manager should be acutely aware of the need to have a specification which describes the service they provide.

Specifications are divided into two parts. One contains the general criteria which govern service delivery. Generally, much of this portion covers good professional practice but in stipulating some of these detail it is possible for budget managers to take advantage of standardised procedures and established best practice.

General principles

These generally include statements which cover the following points:

1. The need for a continued effort to achieve greater service effectiveness.
2. Definition of appropriate staff and support service requirements.
3. Continued improvement in the balance of care in favour of the community.
4. Emphasis on the drive towards equitable access in both resource and service provision.
5 The need to optimise resources in care and treatment regimes and the promotion of modern techniques in prevention, diagnosis, care and treatment (where appropriate).
6. Coordination of service delivery with other forms, ie acute with community etc.

Points to consider

Budget managers must be careful, however, in signing up to a specification which confuses differing objectives. This can happen where an enthusistic purchaser has not been selective in properly articulating vision statements. Evidence of such confusion is sometimes seen when the appropriateness of care, with equity, acceptability, accessibility, efficiency and effectiveness. In some cases, these objectives are not compatible. They actually represent two sides of an information equation where *equity, accessibility, and acceptability are balanced with effectiveness, efficiency, and appropriateness.*

Thus, the closure of an outlying hospital in the interests of efficiency will damage accessibility criteria as far as the local community is concerned. Similarly, there is often confusion where efficiency and financial savings are concerned. As we have already seen, an increase or decrease in case-load does not always mean a reduction in expenditure.

Compliance

Budget managers seek to comply with specifications by completing an internal audit of the activities. Wherever possible, amendments which will facilitate an improved service profile through the redistribution of resources, are identified. Table 3.1 illustrates a small portion of this task.

The table is only a small sample. It shows how there is an ebb and flow in costs and savings. It is not supposed to balance at this stage.

No	Objective	Measures & monitoring	Findings & comments	Financial consequences Spend £k	Save £k
9.8	**Plan of care**				
9.81	Develop protocols				
	To establish plan of care	Protocol already lodged and agreed with purchaser	Standardisation and rationalisation produced savings in process		4.5
9.82	For care review and assessment	Consolidation of existing scheme	For all investment in documentation	1.2	
9.83	To involve client	Formalising current practice	Savings from better communicaion		12.2
9.9	Where appropriate, provision of an interpreter	Liaison with resource centre for sensorily impaired established	Small investment on an infrequent basis	0.5	
9.10	Policy and procedures for open access to files	Preparing neccessary arrangements	Cost limited to	0.2	
10.0	**Discharge planning**				
10.1	Coordinate with all relevant services	Improving liaison with GPs, hospital & community staff	Cost estimated	0.3	
10.2	Review standard of discharge procedure	Liason team has now been established	Cost of specialist team	20.0	
10.3	Develop support in community	Improvements in paramedic and related staff	Upgrading and improved staffing	21.5	
10.4	Develop needs in community assessment arrangements	Formal assessment of dependency levels and requirements in hand	Rationalisation of current practice and standardisation of procedures estimated to make savings		23.7
11.0	**Resettlement plans**				
11.1	Review standards	Home visit and support	Estimated cost	5.0	
11.2	Review arrangements for monitoring plan of care quality	Professional audit and review standards now being discussed	Improved quality of developing better standards likely to produce savings		22.7
11.3	**Terminally ill**				
	Protocols to conform with spec for palliative and bereavement care	Protocols now being assessed and appropriate amendments being made	Cost of this initiative still being evaluated		

Table 3.1. Care of the elderly—specification audit

Competent budget contractors

Budgetary contracts are best located at a suitable optimal level. However, with the changes in service delivery, this needs to be reviewed as part of the whole process. The decision about where these should be allocated must always be dependant on factors which limit the range, size and scope of service levels.

The selection of budget managers is a delicate matter and must be handled with sensitivity. Determination of where authority and responsibility must be placed should be subjected to a logical process. The stages of this process together with the considerations to be taken into account are shown in Figure 3.3.

In a paper 'Limiting factors in budget contracts'[1], I discussed the various issues which pertain to the delegation dilemma. These are mainly concerned with the size of a budget and the amount of authority and responsibility which will be delegated. Having resolved the delegation dilemma, through the selection of budget heads already described, it is important to be clear about how future funding, particularly in connection with inflationary pressures, will be managed. The methodology to be applied here is 'considered rigidity spectrum application' (see Figure 3.4).

Where large-scale spending is either planned or executed, it has been seen that the control and management of expenditure within the limits of available income is not a comprehensive objective. Budgetary management is also concerned with public accountability. This implies much more than simply living within available resources. Budget managers, working within the confines of their contract, are expected to apply judgement to how public money is expended. They are also expected to render an account of the expenditure they have incurred.

Stage	Consideration
Budget size	• Maximum delegation means: – more budget holders – smaller budgets • Longer budgets means: – fewer budget holders – greater flexibility
Viability	Make compromise between maximum delegation and flexibility: this will produce a spending range which can be managed
Short list potential candidates	List all candidates and decide competence required
Budget system	Test short list against proposed system
→ Decide	

Figure 3.3. Considerations in selecting a budget manager

They must be seen to properly participate within the authority's regulations and to ensure consistency in obtaining the best value for money for the goods and services they obtain. A public authority's organisation and structure will be designed according to its needs. Budgetary management and communication must be compatible with this design, although evolving hierarchy may result in a number of management tiers.

The key items that managers will wish to see in their contract are:

- What is the main objective workload?
- When has the objective to be achieved?
- How much is allocated for the task?
- What quality and quantity of resources can be purchased for this amount of money?
- What performance criteria will be used?

Budget management implementation

From the 1950s to the 1980s, most public services enjoyed significant growth. Thereafter, although growth has continued, the way in which some services were managed and delivered changed. The advent of competition and the encouragement of the mixed economy has presented a considerable challenge which budget managers must respond to. Their role has therefore changed from a holding situation—holding finances in check—to one of actively marshalling and positively managing resources.

The change from a mainly passive role to a more dynamic interventionist capacity is a potent characteristic which must be clearly understood and fostered. Competition has exaggerated the demand for quality value-for-money services. The significant change in culture has created a hither to unknown environmental awareness. This awareness is applied both internally and externally.

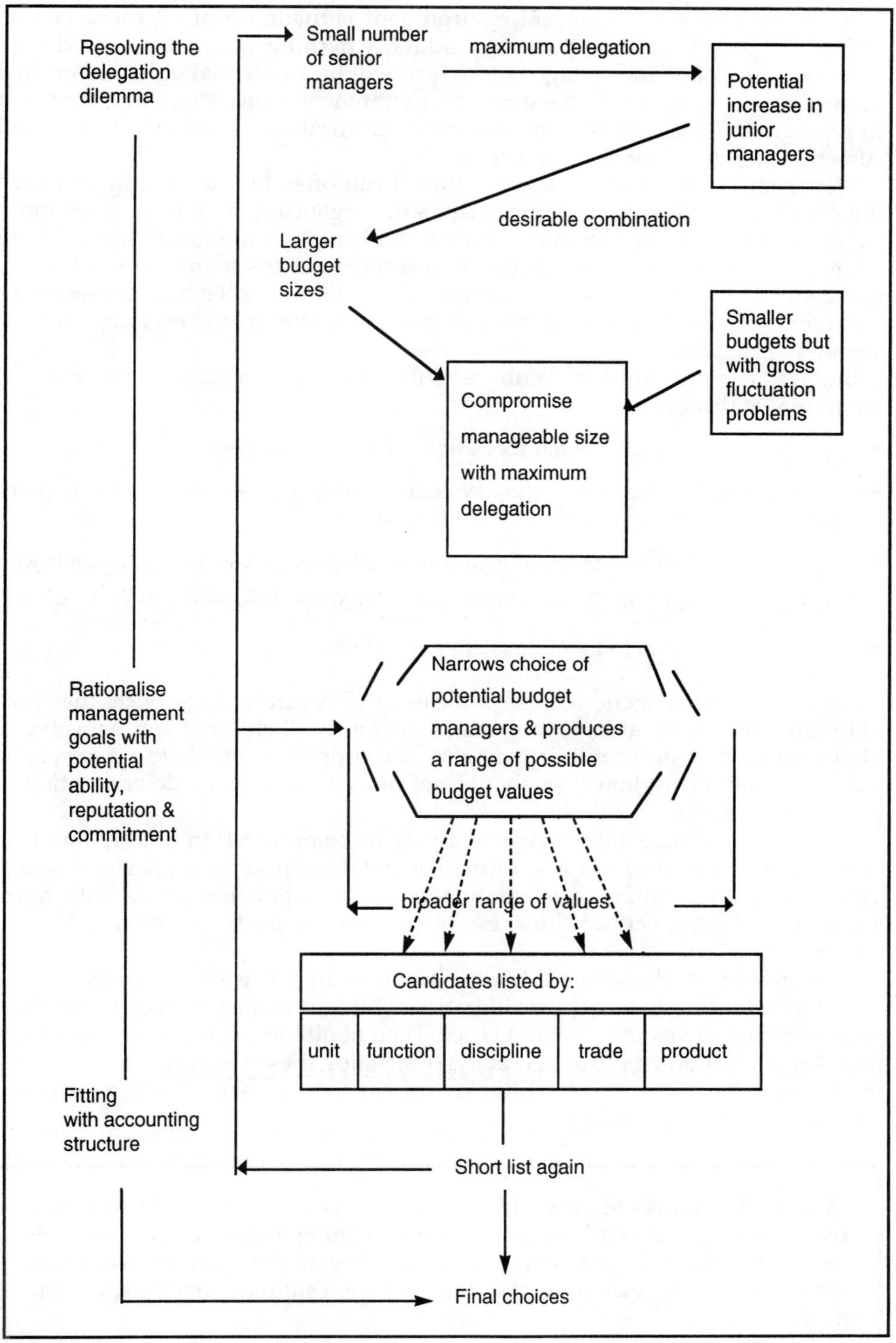

Figure 3.4. Contractor selection process—'considered rigidity spectrum'

A budget manager's external environment is made up of all those factors which are perceived to impact the budget. Anything which lies outside the boundary of a particular budget and which will be a potential influence on that budget is said to belong to the external environment. Generally, these are taken to be organisational and system influences, political and financial climates and customer volumes expressed as work-loads.

Management of the external environment can often be successfully achieved through increased profile. In more dynamic organisations this is given more overt exposure through the development and implementation of a marketing strategy. The more obvious objective is to secure an increase in the market share and better resourcing, but subliminal messages concerning the budget manager's confidence and competence attract greater sympathy in the establishment of spending priorities.

Budget managers must therefore carefully target key elements in the external environment through:

- providing an organisational focus upon their achievements;
- maximising the use of spending systems through proper cooperation in planning;
- creating political awareness (large and small 'p') of the value of their service;
- taking account of the financial climate and managing within constraints;
- utilising surpluses to increase customer volumes.

Some budget managers, because of the emotive nature of the services they provide can have an advantage, for example seriously ill children and educational high fliers tend to attract public sympathy and support where there appears to be a disadvantage. This, however, should not reduce a manager's determination to promote excellence.

External environmental management may be commenced in a fairly low key, with the productions of simple information and description of service provisions. This can be later enhanced as confidence and competence grows with more sophisticated prospectuses, business plans, cases, reports, the launch of road shows, etc.

Management of the external budgetary environment is clearly connected to and dependent on external considerations. Budget managers receive all their resources from outside their boundaries. Their ability to manage these resources in a purposeful and productive manner sustains these resources and enables managers to be proactive externally. In this way they are able to match the external demand with a capacity to cope.

'X' said the figures simply did not add up. The treasurer said that in a recent survey, calculations were found by independent audit to be 99 per cent accurate 85 per cent of the time. 'X' said that was not what was meant and in any case what about the one per cent inaccuracy 15 per cent of the time?

Project management in service rationalisation

As part of the effort to increase competitiveness and reduce costs, service profiles must be rationalised. In order to maximise savings, this process must be subjected to careful management. Budget managers must focus upon a number of action points which ensure that the project has direction. Although these will vary from one authority to another in general they may be summarised as:

- Establishing a reliable data base—this ensures that the calculations relating to the cost effectiveness of the project are accurate.
- Market research and consultation—making sure that market shares have diminished to the extent that the retraction is neccessary.
- Obtaining approval in principle—ensuring that all policies relating to this type of action which have been developed or adopted by the authority are being complied with.
- Producing an option appraisal or feasibility study where appropriate—see Chapter 4.
- Carrying out interim negotiations—making sure that all interested parties have received due notice of intent and that they are consulted and informed at all stages.
- Implementing the plan—making sure that the plan is adequately developed and that the activation of the implementation of the stages set out are in accordance with timescales.
- Reviewing the situation.

Tractable complications

Establishing a reliable data base

Fast gathering and the definition of acceptable reference points and periods are essential to planning and implementation of any alteration. This process builds up a factual prehistory position and sets out:

- the historical background;
- the economic case; and
- the perceived and expected quality of care.

Market research

Exploration of the internal market and a general survey of attributes will reveal possible alternatives and the likely reaction from individuals and vested interests. These interests include:

- Patients.
- Relatives.

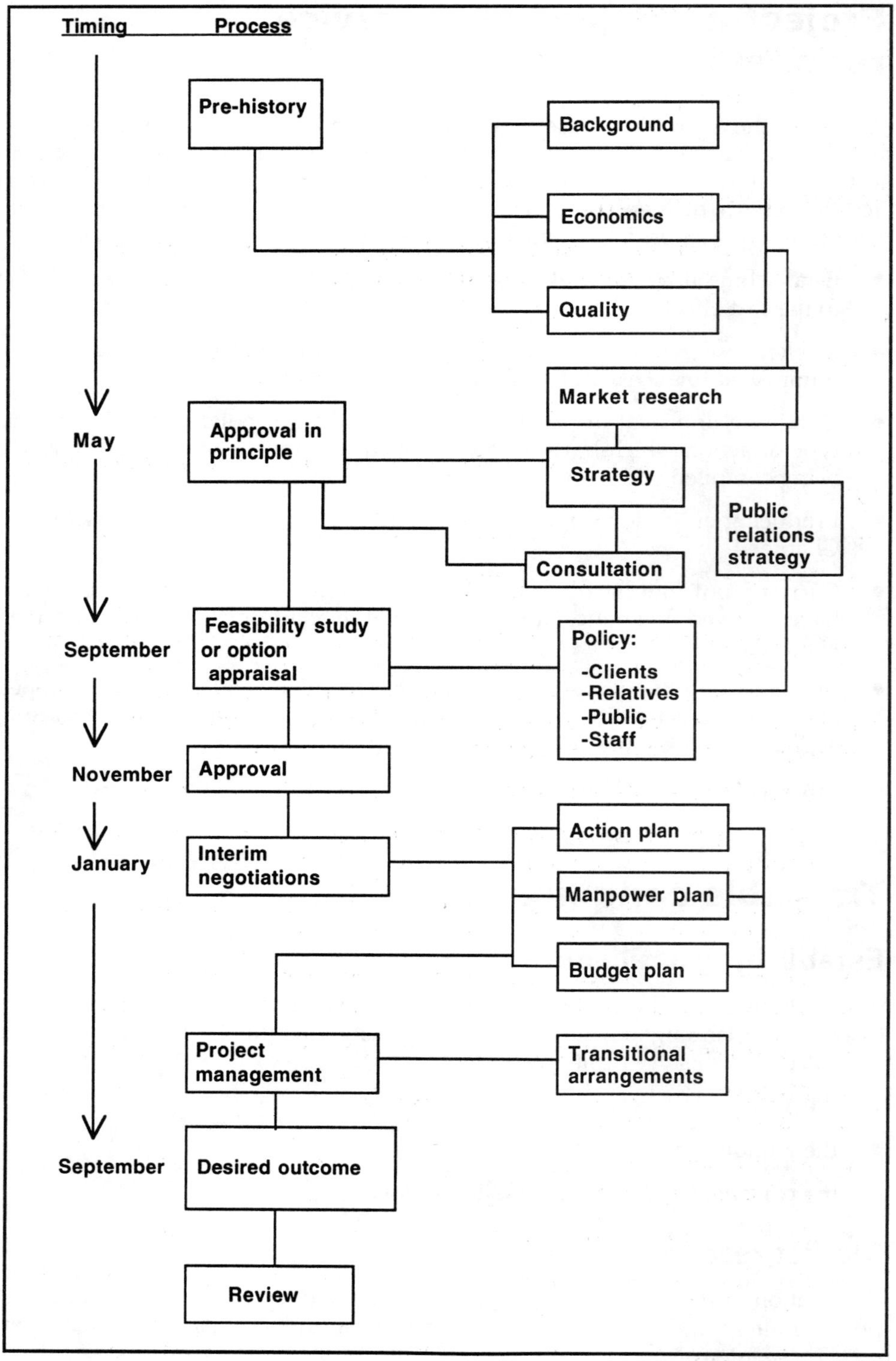

Figure 3.5. Retraction implementation process

- Concerned professionals.
- Staff interests.
- Local pressure groups.
- Media.

Interim negotiations

Interim negotiations follow earlier marketing, consultation and approval of the feasibility study and permits the development of plans for:

- Action.
- Manpower.
- Budget.

This puts into perspective the management of the project and specifies the timing of desired outcomes.

Key points summary

Budget managers in the public services live in a complex environment. This requires them to interact with that environment so that its demands, which may be either the result of natural incidence or may have been self stimulated, can be adequately supplied by them through a process of internal and external management.

- **Definition**—role and scope of managers in their environment.
- **Strategic influence**—how best the manager can react with the environment and what determines mutual influence.
- **Direction**—the broad dimensions which determine how resources can be most effectively used.
- **Competent contracting criteria**—managers need to be aware of and, where possible, participate in the contracting processes.
- **Development**—the control of contracts where there is change.
- **Budget products**—how the delegation of authority and responsibility affect opportunities for planning and control.
- **Management**—prevention and intervention as catalysts for changing expenditure patterns.
- **Business and service profiles**—profiles and marketing.
- **Competition**—the development of the mixed economy and its affect on the budget manager.
- **Performance**—criteria for measurement and opportunities for improvement.
- **Audit**—methodology for service and budgetary audit.

Case study

Following the audit criticism, there was considerable speculation about the award of the budget contract to Hopefields' manager.

The treasurer was concerned that the size of the budget meant that there was little flexibility, and it should therefore be consolidated into a larger grouping of similar facilities.

The Director of Services for Disabled People, however, took the view that with emphasis now quite clearly upon improving facilities available to carers in the community it should remain.

Directors generally, were impressed with the quality and accessibility of the service. Most were agreed that the efforts of Resource Centre staff to increase their income by sales of work was commendable.

The Director of Social Services disagreed with this latter view. She felt that staff should not be concerned with financial pressures because this took up valuable time which would otherwise be devoted to the clients.

It was finally agreed that it was neccessary to draw up a service profile into which a specification that complied with the overall focus of the service. In order to alleviate some of the pressure an increase in the contract sum of £7000pa was allocated. It was noted that this would facilitate increasing the total number of attendences per year to around 7,000.

References

1. Limiting factors in budget contracts, in *British Hospital Management* 1992.

4

The internal environment — budget managers as purchasers

Objectives

The main objective of this chapter is to show how budget managers must behave as purchasers within their own environmental domain. The chapter deals with the nature of financial management as controlled by the budget manager and how best this spending power can be directed as part of an overall strategy. Specifically, the chapter looks at:

- The structure of expenditure and how this is composed of:
  - Capital spending (and how this compares with commercial practice).
  - Non- recurring revenue spending(large items of spend are not regularly replaced).
  - Revenue spending (day-to-day outgoings on a regular basis — such as payroll etc.).
- The effects of resource spending on the stucture of cost with specific reference to:
  - Fixed and variable costs.
  - Marginal costs.
  - Resource categories.
- Establishing resource spending priorities.
- Devices and methodologies used to obtain value for money.
- Feasibility studies.
- Options for expenditure.

The structure of expenditure

The direction of spending on health and social services is the enabling purchasing factor in obtaining value for money, in demonstrating public accountability and in procuring the resources most appropriate to the effective care and treatment of patients and clients. Spending on resources can be described as being:

- Capital — tangible items which are new and/or add to the value of assets.
- Non-recurring revenue — items which are not capital but which have caused extraordinary expenditure.
- Revenue — spending on day-to-day running expenses.

Resources may be divided into six broad categories: expertise; materials; estate; equipment; finance; and systems (EMEEFS).

> **Finance is the most liquid resource and its relationship to the others is expressed in terms of capital and revenue expenditure.**

These resource categories can be split up according to the type of expenditure incurred (see Table 4.1).

Type of expenditure		Capital		Non-recurring revenue		Revenue
Expertise	✗	Not usually	?	Rarely	✓	Always
Materials	✗	Not usually	✗	Not usually	✓	Always
Estate		✓		✓		✓
Equipment		✓		✓		✓
Finance		✓		✓		✓
Systems		✓		✓		✓

Table 4.1. Resource categories by type of expenditure

In revenue terms, health and social services care has a strong service base. This means that a large number of professional staff is required. Hospital doctors, general practitioners, nurses, paramedical and social services staff represent a large part of the work-force. This results in a large proportion of the budget being spent upon payroll. It also means that although other resource expenditure is scattered over revenue and capital, staff costs are almost always in the revenue category.

As an example of the kind of relationship that exists in this complex financial structure, listed below is an estimate of spending on health (hospitals and community) in a scattered rural community which supports a number of medium sized towns. The total population is around 500,000 people.

Spending	medical	nursing	support staff	other revenue	Non recurring	capital	total
£m	30	66	42	41	12	10	201
% of total	15	33	21	20	6	5	100

The relationship is illustrated in Figure 4.1.

In general, the payroll component of health care can represent between 70 to 80 per cent of total revenue expenditure. Bearing this factor in mind, it follows that the management of payroll expenditure is a very large contribution towards gaining overall management. Although the capital values of estate, equipment and systems are often about equal to the yearly revenue expenditure, much smaller revenue amounts in comparison with payroll are incurred in providing for the day-to-day running of estate, equipment and materials.

Experience indicates, however, that the smaller segments which represent the so-called 'other spending' and non-recurring expenditure provide greater challenges. This is due to a number of factors. The main ones are the disparate complexion of these elements taken together with the multitude of demand sources and difficulties in maintaining control of the cost of individual items. For example, the control mechanism to be applied to metered changes such as water and electricity will significantly differ from that which could be applied to general material such as food or clothes. This implies that a system of management must be based on a series of expenditure centres which represent both the totality of the scope and range of expenditure and can clearly be identified with the sources of demand for expenditure.

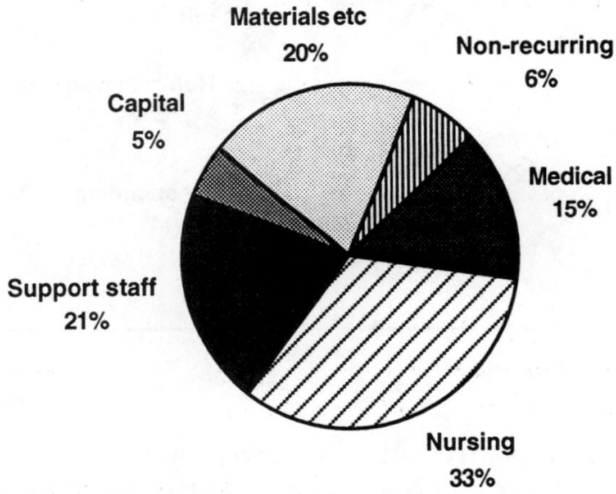

Figure 4.1. Hospital and community unit expenditure

In a situation where the business of an authority remained unchanged the direction of expenditure would be limited only by external factors such as inflation.

The emphasis upon this culture of change, however, means that most authorities have been exposed to a more competitive approach to the way they transact business. During the last decade the promotion of a mixed economy, where more competition is encouraged, has been a prevalent characteristic. Initiatives such as competitive tendering and self governance for hospitals and schools are examples which are claimed to render better public accountability and value for money.

Direction and scope of expenditure

Other initiatives, too, change the direction of spending. In health, there is progress in achieving a better balance of care through shortening the length of time patients remain in hospital, resulting in fewer hospital beds and fewer hospitals. Another example is found in social welfare where there are fewer statutory homes for the elderly and for children. Both these initiatives are complemented by a growth in the private sector and improvements in community care. As well as this there is a continuing focus on the expenditure created by general practitioners.

As far as the total provision (and purchase) of health and personal social services to the community described above is concerned, Figure 4.2 illustrates what the overall position might be.

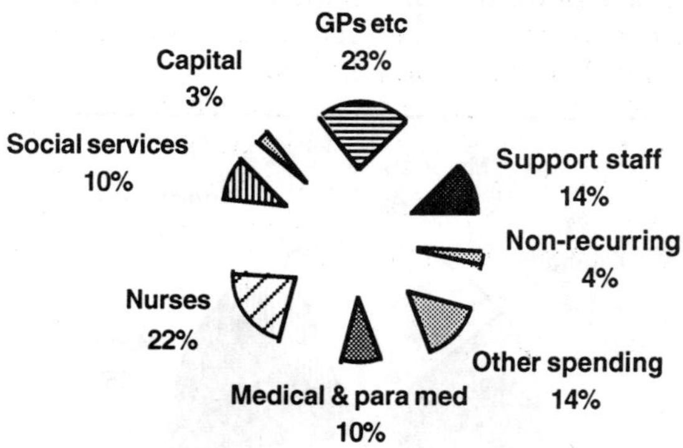

Figure 4.2. Resource allocation model

Although the current initiatives and the power language of business would suggest the contrary, there would always have been a desire to direct expenditure to those areas where it is most needed. In pursuit of this ambition, authorities constantly evaluate their financial position. In addition, the government also seeks to ensure that there is an equitable distribution of resources. To support this objective a formidable range of performance indicators have been developed which identify resource distribution per capita. These may be used centrally or locally to signal the lead for a redirection of finances. This requires a fair degree of sophistication and implies extensive use of budgetary techniques.

The direction of spending is the subject of constant alteration. Some spending areas will gain. Some will lose because of retraction and some will remain more or less the same. The management process requires information which facilitates intervention in the direction of expenditure at both strategic and operational levels.

Capital spending

In the commercial world, the accountant attributes a variety of meanings to the term 'capital'. It can mean the original fund used by a trader to start a business. This is represented by the excess of assets over liabilities. In the case of a joint stock company, it refers to the amount contributed by shareholders. To the economist, capital is one of the factors of production. However it is defined, it is an important resource which is combined with other resources to generate income or benefit.

The cost of capital, apart from the restriction in choice that investment in selected projects implies, is to be found mainly in interest charges and the depreciating nature of the assets which have been acquired. Until the advent of the reform programme, these costs were not borne directly by the health service and managers were not so aware of the need to use this resource wisely and efficiently.

In addition, the accounting system which preceded the introduction of capital charges meant that it was not easy to evaluate the cost of service provision on a comparable basis to that in the private sector. Furthermore, the new system is designed to facilitate the element of competition.

Capital, or fixed assets, is broadly devided between estate and equipment. The definition includes vehicles. Asset registers record data, including the value of each capital item or group of items. These registers are usually computer based and now that they have been set up and validated they are fairly easy to maintain. The valuation of buildings and land is based on independent valuation and is periodically updated to take account of:

- land and buildings disposed of since the last valuation;
- additional capital expenditure since last valuation;
- indexed increases in the value of land and buildings; and
- depreciation of buildings.

Current expenditure on estate and equipment in the unit described earlier might be as shown in Table 4.2.

Detail	**Estate £m**	**Equipment £m**	**Transport £m**	**Totals £m**
Hospitals	**0.2**	**2.9**	–	**3.1**
Ambulances	–	–	**0.2**	**0.2**
Health centres	**0.6**	**0.2**	–	**0.8**
Health clinics etc	**0.3**	**0.2**	–	**0.5**
Administration	**0.1**	**0.6**	–	**0.7**
Totals	**1.2**	**3.9**	**0.2**	**5.3**

Table 4.2. Expenditure on estate and equipment

Fixed and variable costs

In Chapter 1, the clear relationship between average cost and budget was established. Within the revenue cost range there are two factors at work which affect the average cost, fixed and variable costs. As the terms imply, variable costs tend to be more easily influenced. Fixed costs at low productivity rates are a burden on the budget and it is only where outputs increase to the optimum that value for money is obtained. This is illustrated in the case of Hopefields Disability Resource Centre where a fixed cost of £50k affected the overall performance (see Figure 4.3).

Hopefields data

Situation	Number of attendences	Annual cost (£)	Average cost per attendence
Previous position	5,000	100,000	20.00
Current position	6,000	103,000	17.17
Increased transport	7,000	110,000	15.71
Evening respite	8,000	120,000	15.00
Saturday opening	9,000	144,000	16.00
Sunday opening	10,000	168,000	16.50

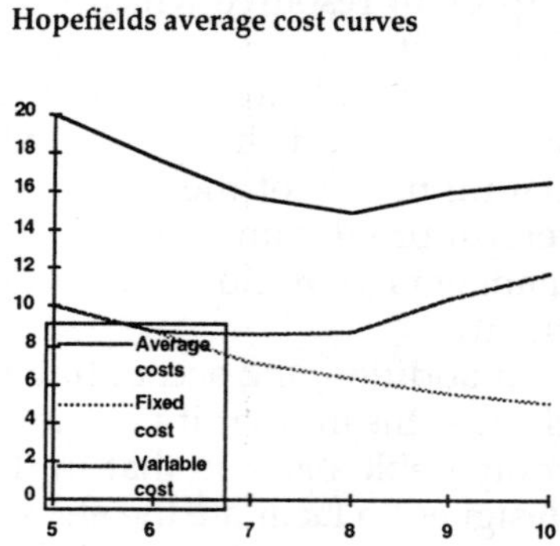

Figure 4.3. Effects of fixed costs on the budget

Improving the prospects

Declining patient/client numbers are found in the occupancy levels for beds or places in the estate generally. Vacant space costs money to maintain and service. Similarly, furniture and equipment usage must be kept under review and where this is found to be unsatisfactory budget managers should take steps to decommission the item. If some new use cannot be found then arrangements for its disposal must be made. These features will be dealt with more fully in later chapters. It is important, therefore, that managers constantly review both the fixed and average cost element in their budgets in order to maximise their potential.

This process examines the current situation to see whether anything of significance has changed that will allow the manager to make better provision for patients and clients. Figure 4.4 shows the position as it was described in Chapter 1; Figure 4.5 shows how an internal saving might be made through a re-evaluation of working practices; Figure 4.6 shows how this saving might be redistributed to facilitate an increase in workload.

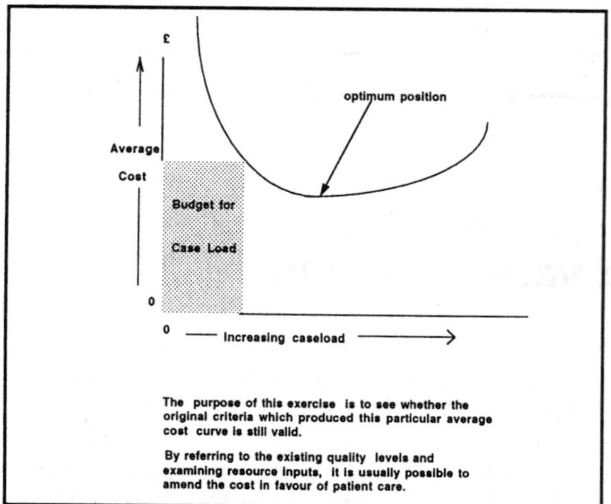

Figure 4.4. Average cost/caseload/budget relationship

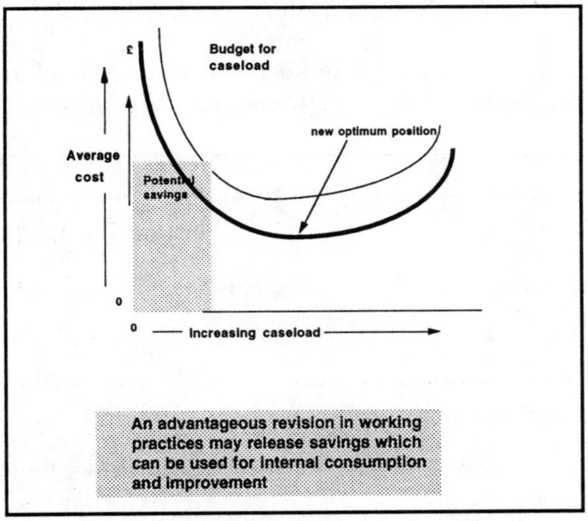

Figure 4.5. Average cost/caseload/budget relationship

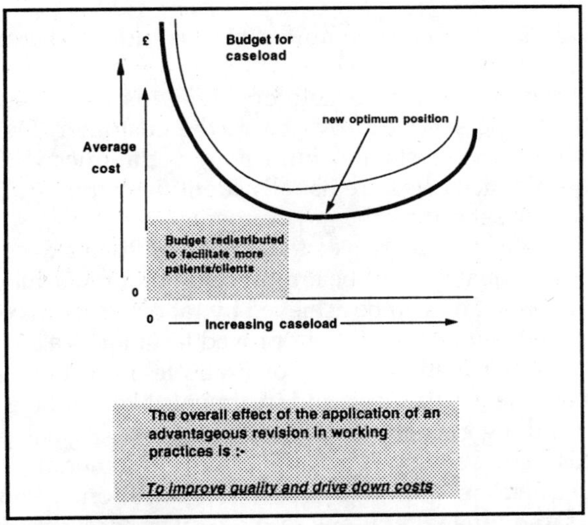

Figure 4.6. Average cost/caseload/budget relationship

The planning equation

In order to achieve a better internal balance there has to be an inherent integrity between the:

- maintenance of satisfactory standards as defined in the application of total quality measurements;
- application of available resources which are limited by expertise, estate, time and finance; and
- acceptable level of customer volume.

A significant shift in one of these factors will have an impact upon the other two. This is usually expressed in terms of cost. However, it is the purpose of management to affect these factors in such a way that standards are improved without disturbing the equilibrium. Figure 4.7 shows how this is achieved.

Line 1	Existing standards	Available resources	Customer volumes
Line 2	Adressing deficiencies	Driving costs down	Improving techniques
Line 3	Developing services		Altering the balance of care
Line 4	Improving standards	Reallocating surpluses	Potential increases

Figure 4.7. Improving standards

Working through this we can see how a plan is unfolded from where we are now (line 1) to where we want to be (line 4).

The existing standard of service delivery depends on the existing available resources and this is the service provided to the customer. Deficiencies in this standard by driving down costs and improving techniques in the way services are delivered. These deficiencies are usually identified from within the organisation. They may also be set out by the government.

For example, the Citizen's Charter or the Patient's Charter documents indicate a number of areas where quality must be improved. In order to achieve this it is necessary to drive down costs. This can be achieved by rationalisation, competitive tender or through better management practice. improved techniques also provide opportunities for better customer management. For example, in health care, emphasis on health promotion and better diagnosis and treatments like key-hole surgery render a greater scope for handling greater volumes of patients at marginal extra cost.

In line 3 services to be developed are identified and generally this is dependant on further cost reductions, although sometimes additional resources are made available. At the same time, alterations in the way services are provided may be contemplated. Again this is also signalled by the government. For example, the community care act favours maintaining elderly people in their own homes as opposed to their admission to residential care. This implies a retraction in statutory places and a development of community care services.

Line 4 indicates the planned position which should be accomplished within a certain time scale.

The budget plan and resources

Arising from this process it is imperative that a robust financial or budget plan is developed to support the business objectives plan. Plan making involves matching strategic and operational demands so that resources are made to equal demand in total terms.

Inevitably, initial or perceived demand will exceed available resources. Further discrepancies will also arise both from impact from inflation and from deficits in the achievement of certain targets. This latter aspect can be due to either difficulties in spending regimes or inadequate funding.

Conceptually the financial plan sets out in broad terms:

- what has to be done; and
- what the organisation wishes to do.

It then attempts to reconcile any deficits which may occur between the financial forecast and the resources perceived to be available.

In forecasting for a particular period, the organisation must take account of:

- Current financial trends.
- Impact of inflation.
- Cost of proposed developments.
- Effects of cost reducing measures.
- Shifts or alteration on the balance of service provision.

The contemplated spending cycle is therefore dictated by these considerations.

Establishing resource priorities

Although a change in spending direction may be established by political and economic circumstance, budget managers need also to be aware of the significant impact resources other than finance have on spending targets. As has been demonstrated earlier, resources such as estate, equipment and manpower are expensive both to purchase and maintain. Repairs and replacements can be extremely costly and sometimes where replacement is contemplated availability may be limited. This is particularly true where specific expertise is required.

Budget managers must ensure that they are properly informed regarding the age, use and usefulness of these commodities.

In manpower which absorbs as much as 70 per cent of the revenue budget, a normal age profile is compared with one which would give rise to concern. This phenomenon is illustrated in Figure 4.8.

There is an abnormally high late peak in the age profile shown in Figure 4.8. This would be similar to that experienced by many public authorities during the 1970s/1980s. High level recruitment of ex-service personnel at the inception of the welfare state brought many such staff to retirement age during that period.

For the experienced budget manager, this can provide an opportunity over a ten-year strategic planning period to restructure. It can also provide for a desirable early retirement programme if a restructuring is neccessary.

The possible disadvantage is that the greater number of older staff in a particular category might mean that the incidence of sickness and injury may increase.

The condition of estate and equipment can also have an impact. In Figure 4.9 building maintenance costs are seen to multiply in a ten-year cycle.

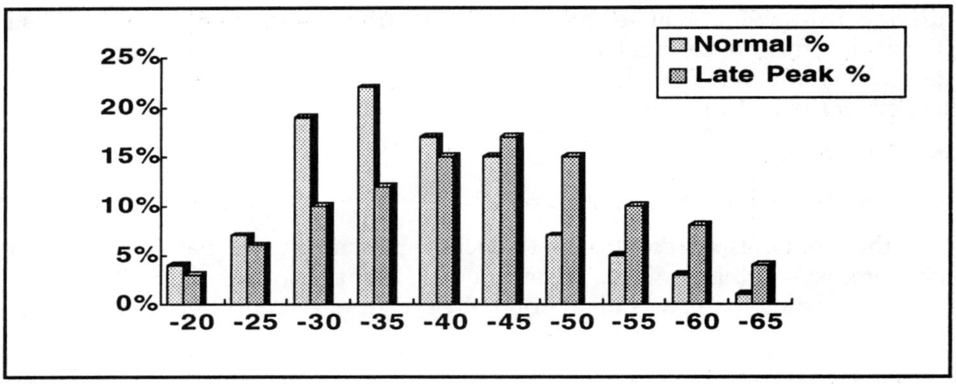

Figure 4.8. Staff age ranges

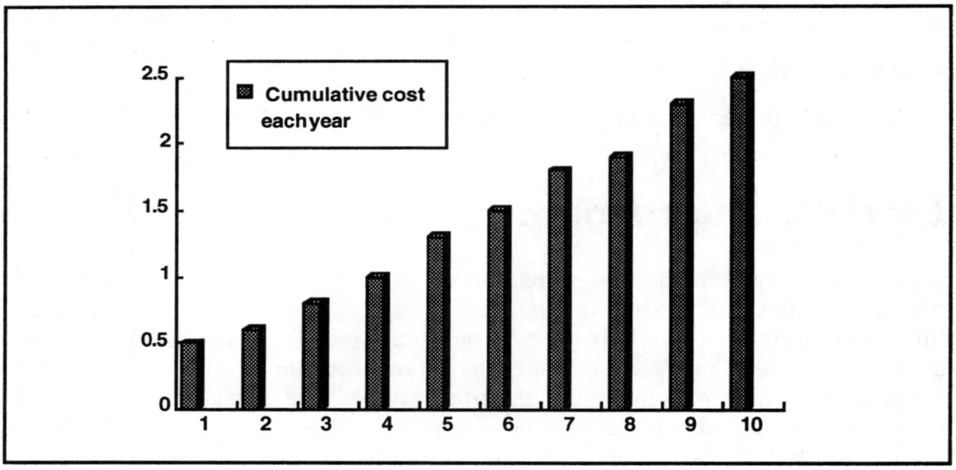

Figure 4.9. Cumulative cost of repairs over a ten year cycle

During the last five years there has been a consistent increase in works expenditure. If further repairs and improvements are required some evaluation is necessary.

The use of estate and equipment is another factor which budget managers must consider. Where use and usefulness has been seen to significantly reduce either as a result of improved techniques or changes in population.

Where a significant purchase of service provision or estate or equipment is necessary, budget managers have to make choices. They have to look at the options and the costs. The feasibility of continuing use must be examined

These examinations are most successfully undertaken by using project management techniques. They should utilise appropriate and accepted methodologies. Generally the processes are broken up into various stages and need not be unnecessarily protracted.

Purchasing decisions which are based on answers to questions such as:

- Is the purchase necessary?
- Can we rent or hire?
- Can we subcontract?
- Is it feasible to change the use and/or rationalise existing arrangements?

are discovered through the correct use of these methodologies.

Looking at the choices

The rationale used in making a purchasing choice is common to all types of purchase. Whether the final outcome is to decide about future purchases of patient or client care, or whether it is to be a decision about the estate or equipment, there is an accepted structure to the way this happens.

> **The purchaser must reconcile a range of options with cost and benefit criteria.**

Options

Main Purchasing Options	1 Do nothing	2 Do minimum	3 Rationalise	4 Rent or lease	5 Share or contract out	6 Purchase

Occasionally the project team or the authority may set out some definitive guidelines concerning which options must be excluded. For example, in the case of the purchase of large-scale equipment, it is generally considered that leasing and the utilisation of the private sector options are unconventional financing methods and are not used except where the proposal offers best value for money.

Acceptability criteria

Some purchasers confuse acceptability criteria with core values. For example, accessibility is sometimes confused with equity and the latter included as either an option or as a part of the acceptability criteria.

Main acceptability criteria	1 Ability & accessibility	2 Efficiency factors	3 Effectiveness	4 Safety	5 Flexibility

Again, there may also be some constraints on the range of acceptability criteria available.This is referred to as specific rejection criteria. For example, acceptability to patients or clients may be a reason for de-selecting a particular option.

Cost criteria

Cost criteria	*Decisions*
1. Approach to costing needs agreement:	• **Budget limitations.** • **Exclusion of exceptions (ie leasing).** • **Define how protocols will be applied.**
2. List any assumptions:	• **Basis of any estimated costs.** • **Where leasing costs are included the valuation method used.** • **Any likely residual values.**
3. Income to be derived:	• **Income generation from increased market.** • **Savings to be made from implementation.**
4. Implementation costs, including works:	• **List all relevant factors.**
5. Increased staffing costs:	• **Staffing consequences must be evaluated.**

Feasibility studies

A feasibility study is generally carried out where a change of use or a rationalisation is contemplated. Its need is generated usually by the supposition that some or all of the factors mentioned are present. An authority will usually commission a group of managers to carry out a feasibility study. The terminology will be general in nature:

- 'to examine services provided at . . .;
- to consider other more satisfactory ways in which these services could be provided; and
- to achieve significant savings.'

The study group's agenda will follow a pattern:

1. **Service profile:**
   - description, location, and catchment population;
   - type of resources, their age and condition; and
   - costs.

2. **Service provision**
   - details of services provided; and
   - performance statistics.

3. **Staffing levels and the implementations of any change.**

4. **Description of estate:**
   - its size etc;
   - investment requirements; and
   - current and potential use.

5. **Opportunities and alternatives:**
   - internal solutions;
   - external solutions;
   - effects upon customers; and
   - manpower plan.

6. **Savings arising.**

7. **Recommendations.**

When the authority accepts the proposals contained in the study, it is usual to record appreciation of staff dedication and justify its decision by underlining the following points:

- Climate of scarce resources.
- Increasing priority commands.
- Need to examine efficiency and effectiveness.
- Need to secure services which are most appropriate to user demands.
- Emphasise the increased availability of resources released from closure, ie deployment or rationalisation are vital for other more necessary priorities.
- Even in a climate of resource plenty, it would be necessary to consider service and reliability.

Key points summary

- Although budget managers are providers, in order to survive they must exhibit purchasing acumen.
- They must derive maximum benefit from their spending power.
- They must distribute their resources in a cost effective way.
- Detailed knowledge of their spending capacity and structure is essential.
- They must become expert in manipulating
  - *capital spending;*
  - *non-recurring revenue spending;* and
  - *day-to-day outgoings on revenue expenditure.*
- By driving down fixed and variable costs they can release savings for service improvement.
- As the cycle progresses, budget managers can measure the consequences of retraction development on stable budgets.
- Thus enabling them to adjust budgets so that the savings generated from retraction can be properly redirected to meet deficits and to develop services.
- They need to establish resource spending priorities.
- They must use correctly facilitating devices and methodologies used to obtain value for money.
- They should become competent in examining options for expenditure and using feasibility studies to establish resource utility.

Case study

An option appraisal will generally be undertaken where a contemplated investment in new or replacement estate or equipment exceeds a certain amount. Sometimes spending limits may be as low as £50,000. It differs from a feasibility study in the intense way costs and benefits are evaluated. Having clearly established the need for the continuation of the service, which depends on the investment, a long list of option's are identified together with a general evaluation of each option's consequences. The long list will usually include extreme options such as nothing → submit the total service to competitive tender. Some of these options will be rejected according to stated criteria.

Short-listed options will then be subjected to a scoring mechanism which weights various non financial benefits. An example is shown in Tables 4.3 and 4.4.

Benefit criterion	Weight	Option 1	Option 2	Option 3	Option 4
Capability	40	5	6	9	9
Capacity	10	6	6	8	8
Acceptability	10	4	4	7	7
Safety	20	4	5	7	7
Future development	5	4	4	7	8
Ease of implementation	5	10	9	1	1
Business strategy	10	2	2	9	9
TOTAL	**100**	**35**	**36**	**48**	**49**

Figure 4.3. Criterion weights and option scores

Benefit criterion	Option 1	Option 2	Option 3	Option 4
Capability	200	240	360	360
Capacity	60	60	80	80
Acceptability	40	40	70	70
Safety	80	100	140	140
Future Development	20	20	35	40
Ease of Implementation	50	45	5	5
Business Strategy	20	20	90	90
TOTAL	**470**	**525**	**780**	**785**

Difference to Option 1

Option	1	2	3	4
Benefit Score	–	55	310	315
Benefit %	–	12	66	67
Ranking	4	3	2	1

Table 4.4. Total weighted benefit scores

Case study — contd.

When these non-financial benefits are compared with the costs of each option in rank order, an inverse relationship often occurs as shown below:

Options	Benefits	Costs
1	4	1
2	3	2
3	2	3
4	1	4

In other words, Option 1 is the lowest cost but it also is the least beneficial. Conversely, Option 4 is the most preferred option but it is also the most costly. A further process which will take into account sensitivity of service requirements is therefore necessary and if cost differentials are small Option 3 might succeed.

Part 1 summary

Budgetary management tasks are performed at different levels in the organisation. These are influenced by external factors such as climate etc. Performance requires budget managers to behave as both purchasers and providers. They can best accomplish this by using a variety of devices and methodologies. Through these processes, budget managers develop the facilities which enable them to make sensible strategic decisions. They underpin these with financial or budget plans. Budget managers influence factors that lie outside their boundary through competent contracting. Acquisition of the requisite skills enhance their reputation and the attraction of custom and funding. Their greatest impact will be upon the effective use of resources directly within their span of management. Budget managers make use of their acumen, the organisation and the system to enhance their resources. Through this process they are empowered as budget managers. It is the task of budget managers to meet the objectives that they have developed and have set at strategic level.

Part 2

Synopsis—Operational management and tactical intervention

The internal management of allocated resources by the individual budget manager is a continuous process. It involves constant management of income and expenditure.

Continual monitoring and appropriate intervention is necessary in order to achieve these objectives.

The first step is to assess the share of resources allocated to the budget manager. This will include consideration of the range of income options available to the manager.

- Achieving agreement upon the nature and scope of expenditure to be undertaken within the limits, and initiating this activity.
- Measuring the effectiveness of action.
- Intervening at appropriate times to ensure compliance with objectives.
- Controlling activities to ensure that spending is contained within income.

The structure and direction of Part 2 is shown below:

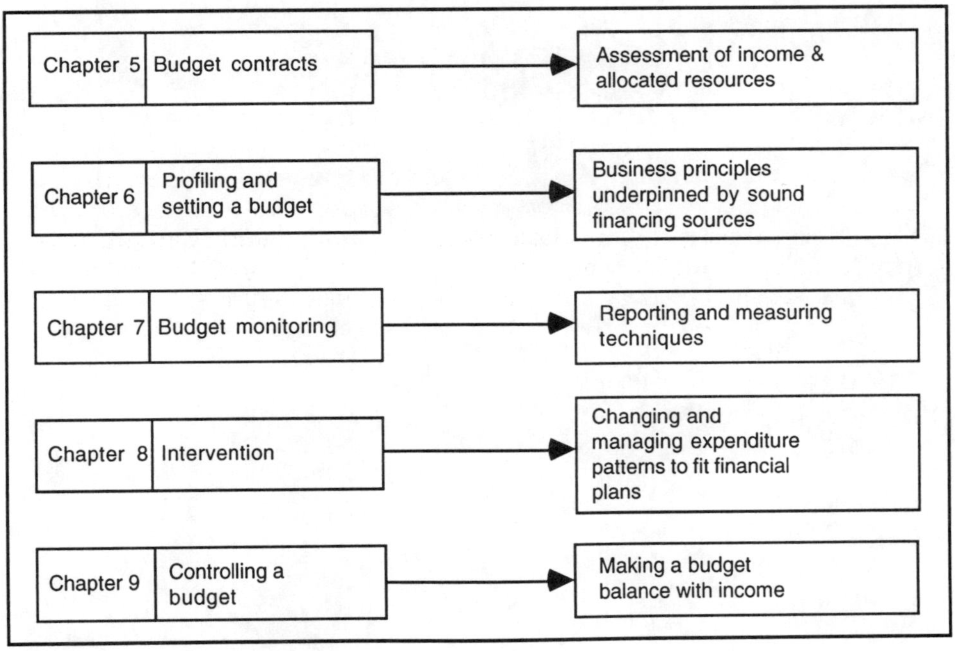

These elements, together with the influencing factors discussed in Part 1, are the key issues that have to be considered when measuring performance. This is the subject of Part 3.

5

Budget contracts

Objectives

Budget managers have an inherent problem when they try to meet the demand for their services from the scarce resources that are allocated to them. In order to maintain their supply they have to create realistic shopping lists and make bids at appropriate times on funds as they think these might become available. The purpose of this chapter is to show how individual budgets are related to the income available and how their performance is constrained by the limitations imposed by the condition of other available resources. The chapter considers the role of budget managers as:

- Income generators through main contract participation and other sources of income.
- Income distributors over the range of necessary resources by constructing 'shopping' lists.
- Bidders for additional funds to enable them to maintain their services.

The chapter deals with the range of income options that are available to budget managers, the limits that constrain the use of these options and how the demands of other resources cause or influence the disposal of this income, specifically the use of:

- Business reviews.
- Market and income plans.
- Contracting for custom.

These features determine how the budget manager will plan spending. It is important that these matters are fully understood because they are the foundation for the planning, monitoring and controlling mechanisms.

Scope for improvement

It has already been seen how budget managers obtain a strategic direction. This is underpinned by a financial or budget plan which translates this direction into monetary terms. In order to have attained this position the budget manager will already have been proactive in the external environment and will have had some part to play in the overall planning and contracting process. Individual budget plans which reflect that particular budget's share of income must therefore be developed within the parameters which have been agreed.

The more *conventional* types of income will be familiar to most managers:

- Income from main purchasers derived from major contracts—this is specifically for the provision of services specified.
- Receipts from private patients.
- Legitimate sale of goods within the budget manager's domain through trading—restaurant receipts, laundry income, etc.
- Disposal of capital assets.
- Allocations from free or endowment funds for both revenue and capital purposes — this type of funding is particularly prevalent where a hospital has a long tradition of service to the community or where the service commands a substantial public sympathy and support.

In addition, a local community will often raise money for specific purposes—recently, scanner appeals have become popular. The danger with this type of initiative is that the cost of accepting, commissioning and running the gift can be substantial. It is important that local goodwill is properly fostered at the outset and channelled at an early stage into projects which will be mutually beneficial.

The shaping of public opinion and the generation of useful goodwill is part of a managers's role when managing the external environment.

There are also a large number of *less well known* funding options. In this context, the use of the voluntary, academic and private sectors must not be ignored. These are particularly relevant to pilot projects but in certain larger schemes, joint funding may be advantageous. These can be split into six categories:

- **Bridging finance**—this is sometimes granted in the form of a loan and is often available to facilitate retraction and the shift in emphasis towards care in the community.
- **Loan schemes**—this method of financing has been available to other public corporations for many years and is familiar territory to those with a local government background. It is usually undertaken with the private sector where normal commercial arrangements prevail. There is, however, only limited powers to engage in this type of arrangement, for example Trusts, and managers should take care when contemplating this method that they conform in all respects with *ultra vires* rules.
- **Partnerships**—this is often practiced with the voluntary sector where a particular type of expertise is available. It is also a method used to bridge gaps in the management development spectrum so that universities offer their expertise to workplace development and in turn derive benefit from the practical aspects of the partership[1,2].

- **Joint ventures or consortia arrangements**—this is sometimes practiced with another authority where it is desirable to give the venture a degree of autonomy. For example, some of the current supplies initiatives may fall into this category also some developing community care schemes.
- **Charges for hotel services and other amenities**—this would require additional legislation and a considerable increase in bureaucracy to ensure that this was properly collected. However, managers should be aware that not every service provided by them may be free. For example, services provided to private patients, persons admitted as a result of a road traffic accident, people suffering other injuries which might be the subject of an insurance claim, generate costs that may be recovered. I mention these because although most people are aware of these facts the costs won't recover themselves. Budget managers need to know what they are funded for and follow it up.
- **Sponsorship**—most authorities have policies relating to this method. Budget managers should take care to check them out.

The type of income will vary depending upon the particular type of activity in which a budget manager may be engaged. From time to time its volume will also vary depending on the contract.

Budget cycles

Arising from the planning process, it is essential that a mechanism for implementing the plan is also developed. This will be the method used to test the plan and to evaluate progress in achieving financial objectives. The implementation of the budget plan will have to be the subject of control and regular monitoring. Through this management process deviations from the plan can readily be identified and new spending priorities established. Where deviations are significant, the original plan might have to be revised and a new plan developed. An overview of this cycle is given in Figure 5.1.

Clearly the time factor plays an important role in this process. It is important that the prospective budget manager becomes aware of the various behavioural aspects of budget spend within a particular financial period and be sure to submit bids at each opportunity.

Some budget managers will be net gainers and some net losers but they should always run through the checklist to see that they obtain all that they are entitled to.

The individual share of the burden will not therefore be proportioned in equal measure.

Managers are encouraged to enhance their income through developing their trading capacity or through the use of other financing methods.

This is a more acceptable and preferred method for bridging any gaps in funding. In this respect budget managers can sometimes alleviate some of the budgetary pressure created by the funding deficit. They can increase income. This is clearly a preferable option to one which would result in a retraction in the services provided.

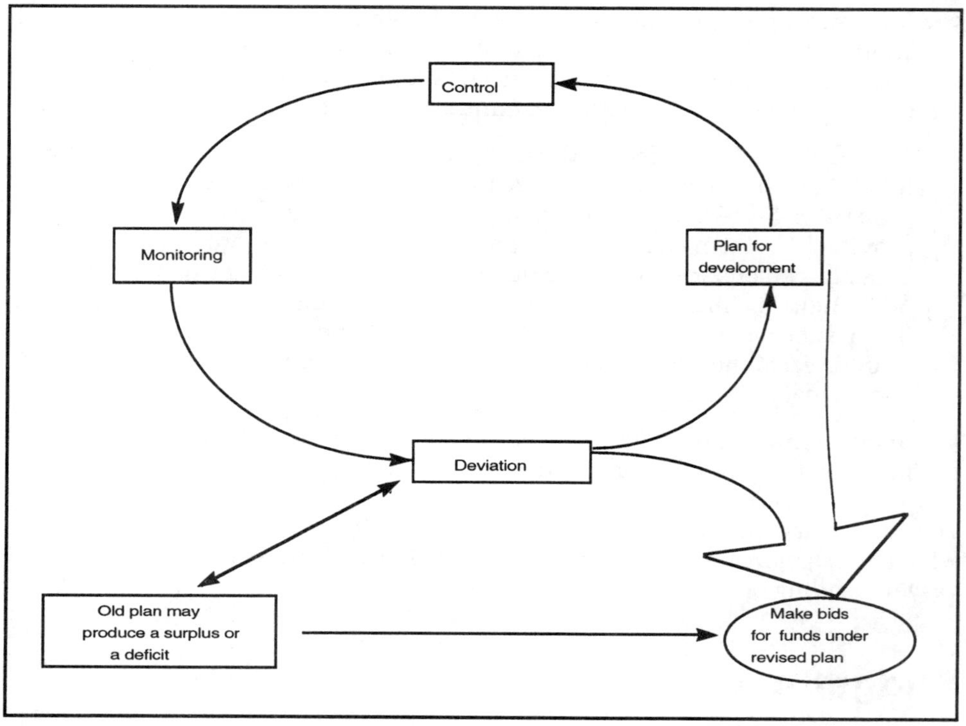

Figure 5.1. Overview of the budget cycle

This trend is likely to continue.

Service providers will seek to enhance their place in the market through a proactive and sensitive response to customer satisfaction. They will tend to share with industry and commerce a dependence on other less conventional income sources for their survival. Trading activities and local arrangements are already increasingly valuable sources.

Generation and control of income derived from main contracts can usually be readily calculated and managed through a central process. This forms the bulk of the present allocations made available to budget managers. However, responsibility for the generation of other additional income is generally perceived to lie with individual budget holders who perform the dual roles of:

- income generators as providers of services; and
- spenders on resources which they purchase.

Business review

Budget managers have to perceive themselves in various capacities—as managers of trading or quasi trading organisations. Trading organisations cover a range of public amenities which are not provided free of charge, for example public transport, leisure amenities, etc. Examples of quasi trading budgets are statutory residential homes, hospital laboratory, catering managers, etc.

In proposing and managing schemes which will generate income, the following management regime can be adopted.

Enhanced income profiles and successful expansion of interests is reflected in escalating financial transactions. An example of a review of business over a number of years is shown in Table 5.1.

Year	Income £k	Expenditure £k	Surplus/ Deficit £k	Net assets (cash, stock & debtors) £k
1	2463	1981	+482	665
2	6309	5331	+978	1643
3	3357	3201	+156	1799
4	3922	4399	+477	1322
5	7727	7069	+658	1980

Table 5.1. Review of business of over a five-year period

From Table 5.1 it can be seen that although income fluctuated over the five-year period, with the exception of Year 4, spending levels were controlled at lower levels thus producing a gradual increase in surpluses. This is reflected by commensurate increases in net assets. The table also demonstrates the fact that actual income received from whatever source is also the budget. It is important therefore that managers develop competence in planning and managing income.

Whatever its source, proper accounts must be kept of all income. Budget holders must take care to observe the standing financial orders of their organisation. No deviation from rules and procedures will be tolerated as they will reflect established principles of good practice.

Income plan

An income plan in the context of trading and quasi trading budgets should have its main objectives:

- Maintenance and improvement of existing income profiles.
- Dissemination of customer information.
- Investment in the promotion of excellence and where appropriate in learning and training activities.
- Business activities which optimise spare capacity.
- Reasonable contingency provision.

In the case of quasi trading budgets there is usually no factual or legal outlet for the accumulating of surpluses. On the other hand, unplanned deficits can only be tolerated within defined limits. Nevertheless, in both cases it is possible to carry out a business review which will give an insight into the existing profile.

Issues which arise from this include:

- the control of demand;
- the acquisition of maximum benefits from sponsorship; and
- the disposal of accumulating assets.

With escalating financial growth, the budget holder should recognise the need to consolidate financial management in the confidence that this trend will continue. Proposes to reduce the financial problems through creating maximum stability in balancing income with expenditure should be made so that there is:

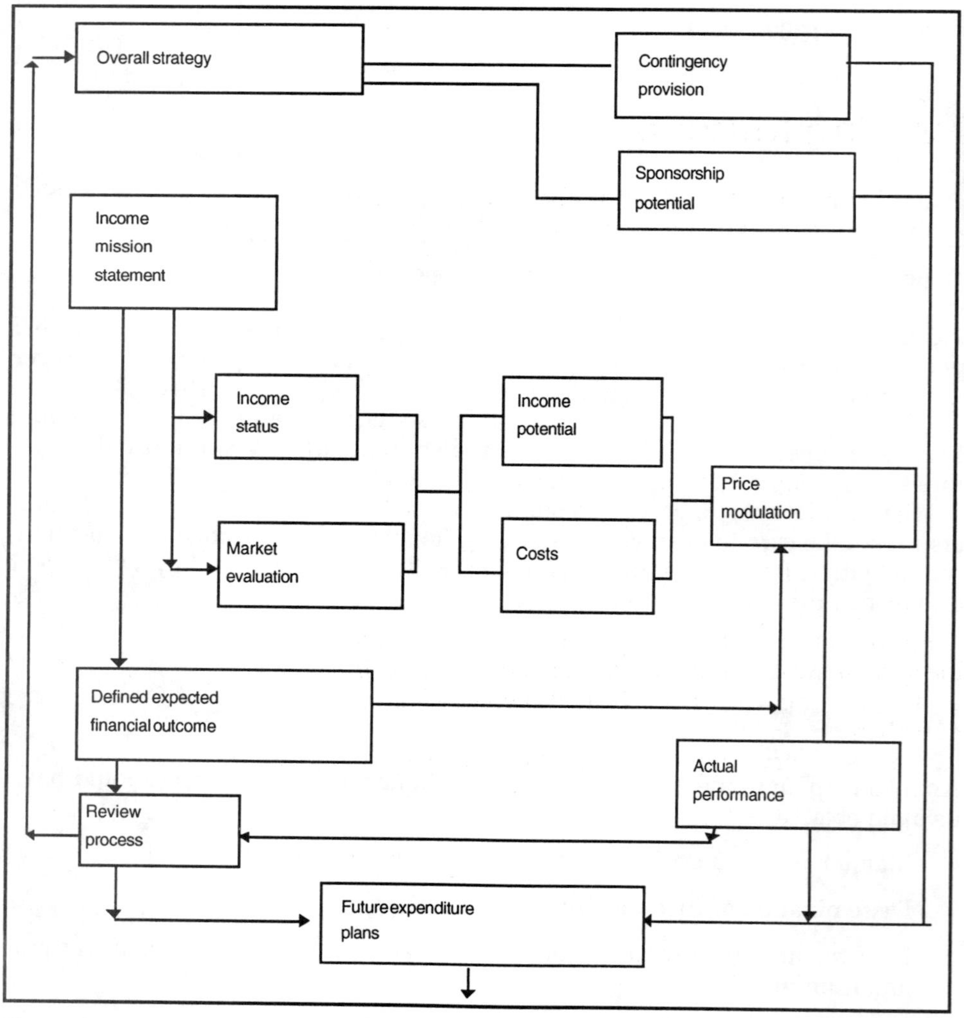

Figure 5.2.

- clear definition of objectives and expected financial outcomes;
- the allocation of specific responsibilities;
- sponsorship initiatives; and
- imposition of price moderation.

The expansion of business must be compatible with the budget holder's profile and in keeping with the legal role. However, where demand is likely to prove greater than available resources it might be necessary to impose controls through the price mechanism.

The development of proper sponsorship contracts could prove beneficial as a method of providing a defined source of income and a security through the adoption of sound business principles. Potential sponsors should be given the opportunity of competing for high-, medium- and low-profile advertising. This should result in the generation of mutual goodwill and should be of considerable financial benefit.

Valuing income

As with any accounting system, the first step is to detect and record the sources from which resources are drawn, these can then be allocated as spending targets. Yet, even in receiving income, the commitment principle applies for this too must conform with expectation and measurement of the flow of funds against an income target is inevitable. Income must therefore equate with spending targets. Negative variations will have a more immediate impact than surpluses, however. Thus the links have to be clearly and firmly established. Commitment strings must therefore be seen to relate to one another both mathematically and physically so that the accounting rules to be applied automatically draw attention to the need to revise spending programmes.

It must be borne in mind, however, that allocation reviews may be due also to inflation or fluctuations in demand for finished products which are not immediately evident in terms of cash flow. This is particularly true to decreases, where stockpiling may be tolerable for a short term.

It is clear, therefore, that each organisation's method of accounting for income will differ in respect of the type of income to be received but it is also clear that the system must be sensitive to fluctuations in the inflow of funds. The difficulty in determining a variation in real income (final cash) is too familiar to dwell upon here.

It takes a very simple view of the cash system. In fact most arrangements would not be so fragile being cushioned against income fluctuations through the skilful management of raw materials and finished articles (if these are appropriate to that particular organisation). This, together with other reserves, is a familiar protective measure but stockpiling in any part of the system is a use of cash and it can be argued that stocks are commitments whereas in financial accounting they would be counted as an asset. In order to make the system work, therefore, it is important that the attitude towards and role of, all reserves are clearly defined.

To some extent these problems are dealt with by the application of commitment principles, which in general terms recognise only the actual attainment of objectives as a measure of success. Thus, while taking account of the

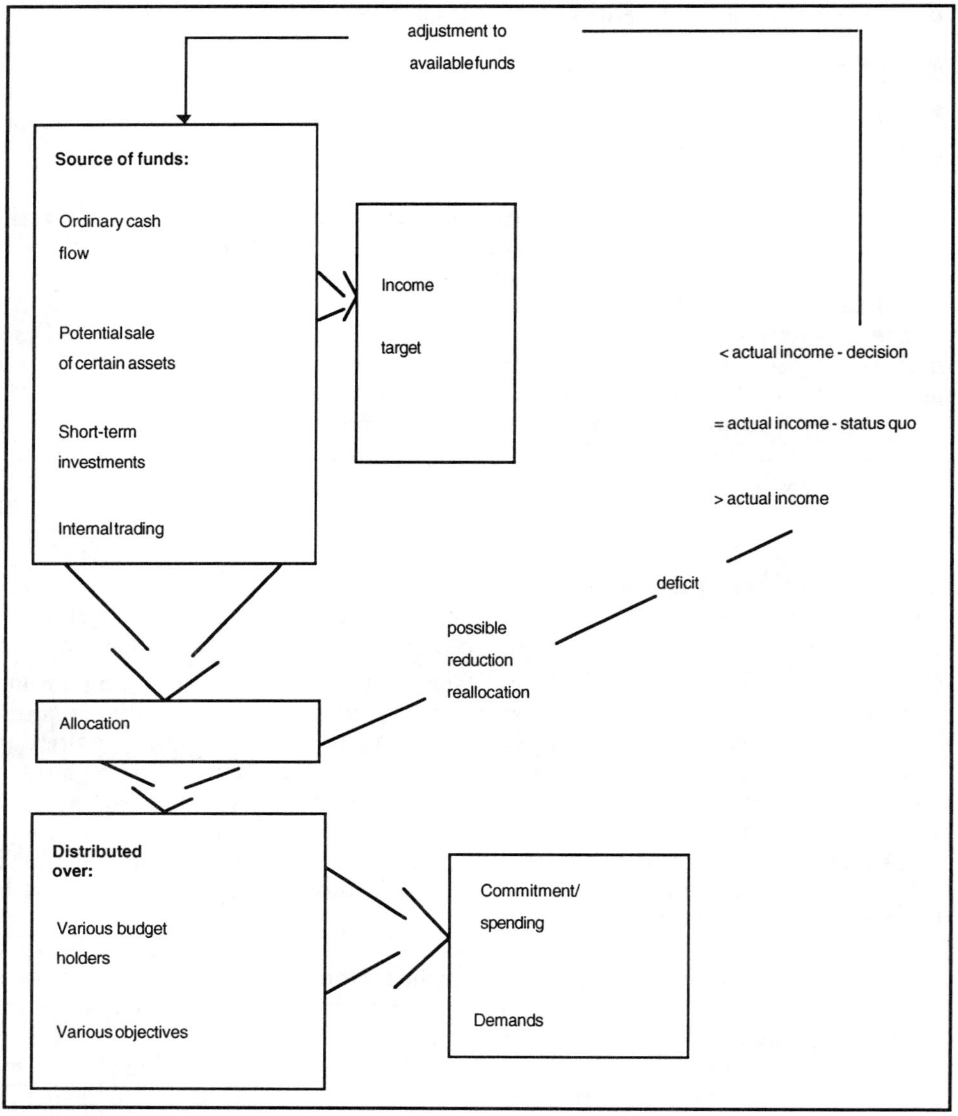

Figure 5.3.

commitment decision, the reality of procurement within the time limit is the objective. If this is not achieved, then the decision is carried into the next time-frame or cancelled altogether. It would be impossible to deal with every variation, but in working through some basic records, the general application will become clear.

The source, level and timing of cash income are primarily set against spending objectives and the cumulative spending against commitments are made compatible with income. In the example in Table 5.2, the expected income is 300 units but the scatter is such as to preclude the use of the total funds in an immediate commitment programme.

Periods	1	2	3	4	5	6	Totals
Source A	15	16	18	19	17	15	100
Source B			20	10	70		100
Source C			10	40	50		100
Column Totals	15	16	48	69	137	15	**300**
Cumulative Totals		31	79	148	285	**300**	

Table 5.2.

In fact, as far as ongoing commitments (like payroll) are concerned, the pattern would not allow continuous or regular spending beyond 15 units or a possible increase to 31 in Period 2. In reality, of course, such short-term fluctuations would usually be covered by some sort of reserve arrangements. However, significant variations are limitations upon opportunities and it could be concluded that while the income target will be made equal to expectation, initial spending commitment will be less than the income target, or, if it is not, commitment itself will be maintained at a lower level.

Price moderation

Although health economists attribute a much broader meaning to the definition of price, in the context of budgetary management, *price is the amount of money paid over by the purchaser.*

The aggregate of price represents income to the provider, and cost to the purchaser.

There are a number of market-place factors that regulate price. They are mainly concerned with the demand created for the service, and the ability of the provider to supply at an acceptable price. In a state of perfect competition, as the price rises, increased supply is more attractive but demand is reduced. These facts are the basis for the classic supply and demand curves illustrated in Figure 5.4.

This means that in acceding to demand a provider can supply at a price which at the very least covers cost. The price mechanism may therefore be simple and straightforward. On the other hand, its structure can be complex and include sophisticated attractions which range in scope from prices which ensure substantial surpluses on service provision for which there is little competition, to lost

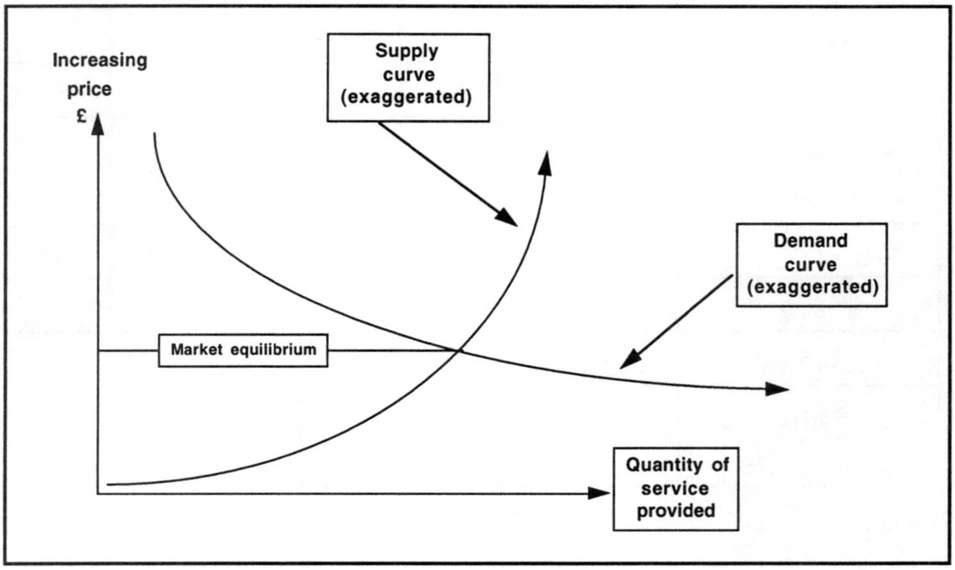

Figure 5.4. Supply and demand curves

leaders where there is immense competition for the supply of a particular service that is in great demand. There may also be a schedule of prices for a range of dependencies.

Where a service, or range of services, is well established but the supply is below the optimum—a situation which has already been explored—management may seek or be persuaded to increase service provision in order to reach the most efficient level of provision. This can result in some debate about the price that should be charged for the increased level.

The amount that is finally agreed should conform to a recognisable rationale. Service providers will wish to acquire a surplus over their true cost but there is often confusion about what exactly the true cost of an expanded service will be.

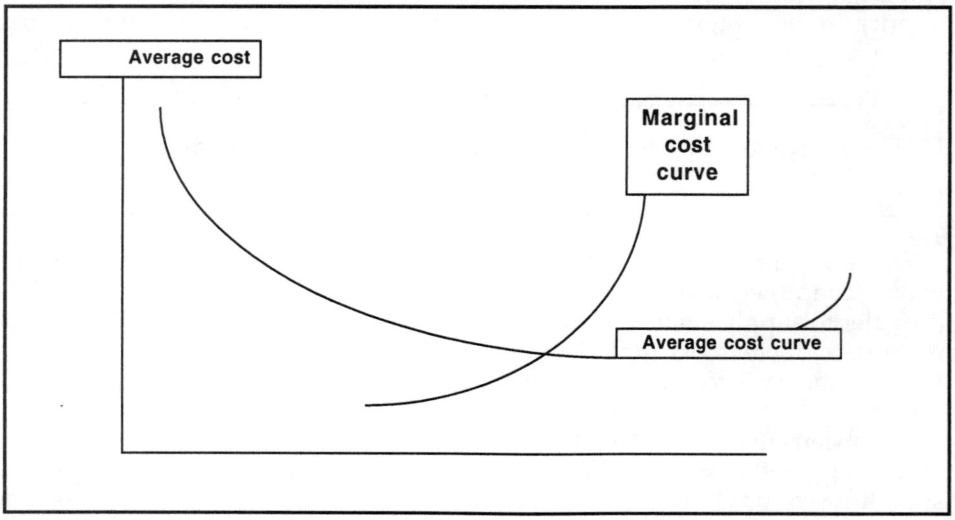

Figure 5.5. Marginal cost

In Figure 5.5 the classic relationship between marginal and average cost is illustrated.

It should be noted that, before the optimum supply position is reached, the marginal cost falls below the average cost. It equals the average cost at the optimum and it is greater than the average beyond the optimum supply level.

In the case of Hopefields Disability Resource Centre the relevant costs are shown in Table 5.3 and Figure 5.6.

Situation	Number of attendances	Annual cost (£)	Increase £	Marginal cost £	Average cost per attnce (£)
Previous position	5000	100000			20.00
			3000/1000	3	
Current position	6000	103000			17.17
			7000/1000	7	
Increased transport	7000	110000			15.71
			10000/1000	10	
Evening respite	8000	120000	**Cross-over**	**point →**	**15.00**
			24000/1000	24	
Saturday opening	9000	144000			16.00
			25000/1000	25	
Sunday opening	10000	169000			16.90

Table 5.3. Hopefields data on costs

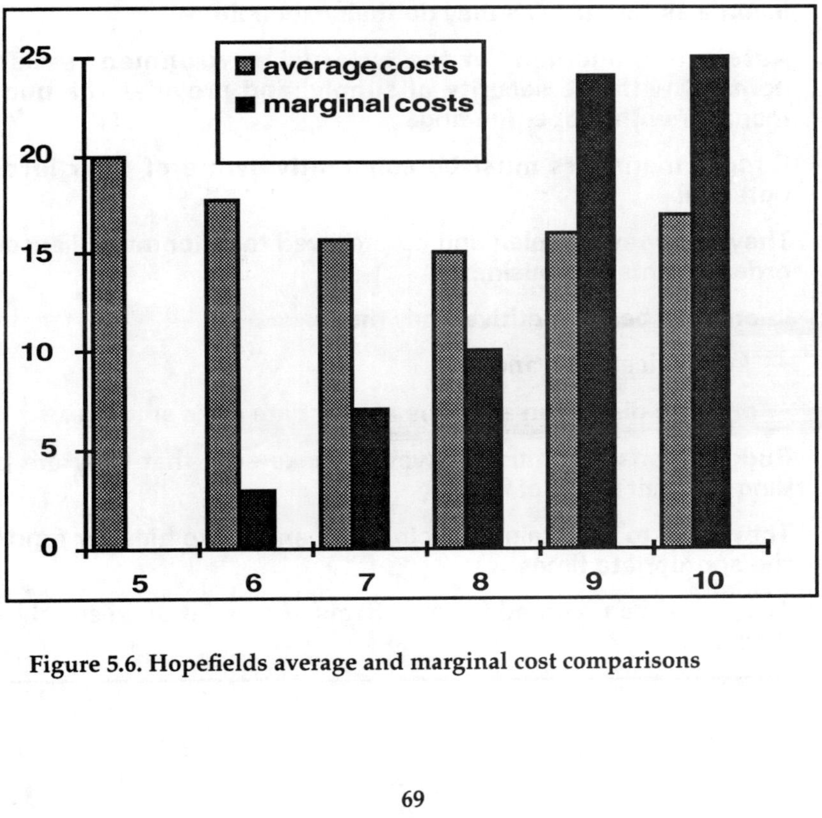

Figure 5.6. Hopefields average and marginal cost comparisons

A newly appointed catering manager was confronted with:

- **low-grade equipment;**
- **a high-risk kitchen environment; and**
- **an inadequate work-place that was causing poor financial performance.**

Money was scarce but this did not deter her from listing all the improvements neccessary to bring the kitchen and her equipment to an acceptable standard.

She explored every income source for works and equipment monies.

She persistently 'did the rounds' of the Treasurer, the Estate Manager, the Director of Support Services and highlighted both the risks and the solution.

Gradually, over a number of years, she obtained piece-meal improvements which, when taken together, amounted to a modern kitchen, food-stores and office environment.

She significantly reduced her costs and, when confronted with competitive tendering, had no problem in getting the contract.

Key points summary

- **Budget managers must be prepared to treat their sources of income as seriously as they do their expenditure.**
- **Astute management of the external environment satisfies demand with the security of supply, and provides the budget manager with proper funding.**
- **Budget managers must be constantly aware of their income potential.**
- **They must review, plan and be prepared to enter into alliances in order to remain in business.**
- **In order to be competitive, they must :**
  - **keep prices low; and**
  - **exercise discretion as to the appropriate price stucture.**
- **Budget managers must, however, make sure that they are bidding for their share of funding.**
- **They have to maintain shopping lists and make bids for funds at the appropriate times.**
- **They must be prepared for the affects of a variation in supply and demand.**

Case study

'X' continued to complain about the level of funding and the Treasurer, recognising a constant irritation, continued to resist.

The Deputy Senior Assistant Treasurer, however, was more amenable to 'X's protests and looked back over the records for the years which preceded attainment of trust status and the recruitment of the presently enhanced senior treasury staff.

It was discovered that the service 'X' provided was the beneficiary of a specific endowment fund which had in the past been used to fund two research posts. In addition, it had benefited from certain grants from free funds to purchase equipment.

The Treasurer was pleased to be informed of this discovery. It enabled an increase to 'X's budget for the current year, but the following year demanded even greater savings on the grounds that the investments from free funds made in the preceding year had enabled 'X' to consolidate and improve the financial base.

Case study

Management at Hopefields had managed to increase the centre's activity from an original position where only 5,000 attendances per year was possible to a capacity of 7,000 per annum.

Marginal costs of £3k for the first additional 1,000 attendances was covered through sales of work. The second 1,000 attendances increase had a marginal cost of £7k and this was funded from Disabled Persons Act monies.

Evening respite would have a marginal cost of £10k and management wished to contract for this as part of the increased range of services to be provided under the community care initiatives.

It was decided that a price of £15 per attendance was more appropriate as this reflected the full cost of an attendance. The Health Authority was not prepared to accept this price and a lower amount of £12 per attendance was agreed.

6

Planning, profiling and setting budget targets

Objectives

Chapter 6 should be read in conjunction with Chapter 5 which was concerned with income origins. The purpose of this chapter is to show how that income is allocated and how we might expect budgets to perform. Specifically:

- How the budget plan is developed from a contract implementation plan.
- Why the various component parts behave differently according to their purpose.
- In what circumstances they must be treated differently by the budget manager.
- When expenditure patterns behave according to time spans.
- How time must be treated as a resource and effectively used according to a manager's competence as a contractor.
- How to avoid wasting time and ways timing is used to achieve objectives.
- How targets can best be set out so that objectives can be met at the right time, first time.
- How the nature of contemplated expenditure tend to dictate a profile development.
- How the budget must be broken up to reflect these objectives at the correct interval.

Contract implementation plans

A contract implementation plan reflects the relevant portions of the main contract. It identifies for the budget manager a number of key objectives which must be accomplished within a particular time frame. The characteristics that may be included in a plan are the:

- identification and redress of any agreed deficiencies;
- development of services;
- retraction or cost improvement programmes;
- confirmation of core service provision;
- arrangements for variable factors such as inflation;
- time-scales for achievements; and
- identification of specific monies to be dedicated to those achievements.

The overall financial plan and individual budget plans for a particular period must be made to balance activities. Because of time-scales and other factors they may not, however, be necessarily synchronised in this way. At any time during the period, the impact of inflation would not be felt in equal measure. Other factors also cause problems. For example, retraction could be delayed or unexpectedly advanced. Similarily developments may encounter like problems.

In the case of retraction, the reality is that where a major programme is planned, investment in service development must come first. This enables the provision of an alternative in advance of the retraction. An example of this is reduction in hospital beds in favour of developing community services.

Sometimes an authority can access central funding sources to facilitate this process. This is called bridging finance and is often made available for a period of years. After this time the extra finance will cease and savings from retraction and cost improvements realised to compensate.

Expenditure patterns arising from the provision of core and other services also behave in different ways according to the period or time-scale being examined. For example, we might expect an increase in holiday relief staff during the summer and an increase in heating and sickness with attendant cost in winter.

During a financial period it is therefore necessary to adjust budget targets so that these expected variations are properly reflected. This process is called profiling and setting budget targets.

Time as a measure of progress

In the complex multi-activity organisation, timing is an essential measurement of efficiency. Problems arise when either, time begins to run out or when it is in over abundance.

- The first is an example of physical objectives unattained.
- The second, a case where there are too few resources to cope with a lengthy time span.

While the expiring time limit can therefore constitute a considerable challenge to organised activity, it may at the same time be a welcome sign of survival. These conflicting facets are manifested in various timing characteristics and are the features that enable time to be made more flexible and manageable.

The time continuum is in itself a perpetually wasting resource. It is also a medium against which events are measured and objectives attained. Each event in a budget cycle may be made to coincide within the same time span, thereby enhancing the value of the time available.

It may be possible to introduce other resources to compensate for a lack of time—buying time.

There are, however, circumstances when this sort of substitution is not possible, and can neither hasten or delay an event like, for example, the advent of harvest. In this situation nothing can be done to change the sequence of the seasons.

These characteristics may be summarised:

- Expiring time limit can be either an advantage or a disadvantage.
- Other resources may sometimes be used to compensate for time shortages.
- Time provides a ready method of measuring progress.

In the budgetary sense it can be seen that time exhibits some features which are similar to certain facets of financial management. Broadly stated these embrace the creation of a harmonious relationship between resources. This is usually done through the definition of a variety of time frames within which it is intended to operate. These artificial time limits can be used as a frequent measurement of both activity and achievement.

Their management, however, will differ in response to the particular kind of expected expenditure behaviour pattern. The expenditure type will also dictate the length of the time span and whether it will be part of a wider spectrum. For example, money made available for one specific purchase would mean that the allocated time frame would stand on its own whereas repetitive expenditure can be examined against small increments of time such as weeks or months, which are themselves miniatures of a larger time frame.

The financial budget, in terms of the time frame, can, in the case of a singular activity, be expressed as a unity. For example, spending on non-recurring or capital items.

In the case of continuous expenditure, the allocation for each miniature will be an increment of the overall total.

These are simple examples of two applications: there are in fact five basic types of pattern which affect timing. They are:

- Continuous predictable—day-to-day spending.
- Development/retraction modes—significant changes in budget direction.
- Casual expenditure—occasional spending.
- Infrequent but predictable expenditure—planned but irregular spending.
- Profiled expenditure—mainly seasonally-related spending.

See Figures 6.1–6.5 for examples of the above types of expenditure.

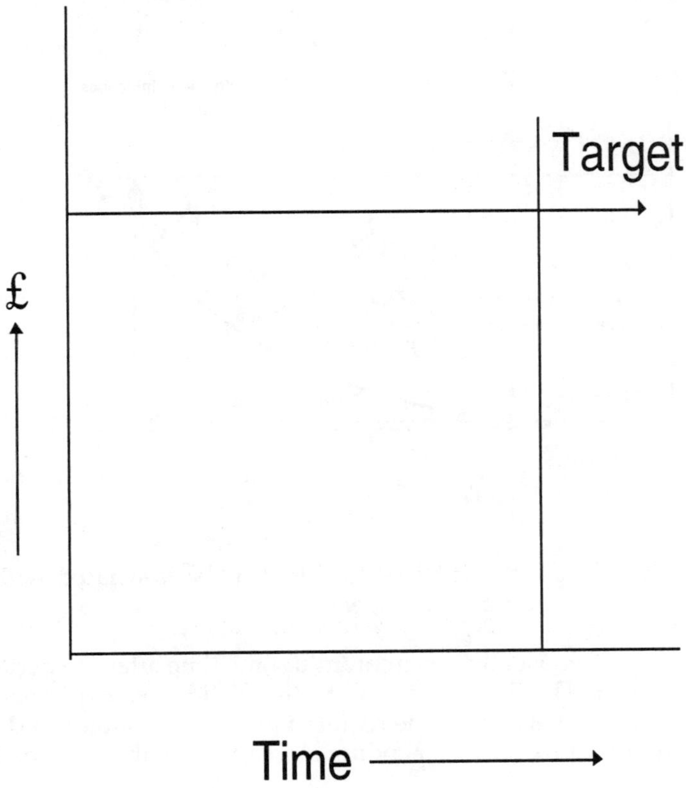

- These types of budgets represent over 70 per cent of revenue expenditure. It is a popular concept of how a control application actually works.
- The basic on-going series of expenses which, although related to the overall cost curve behaviour in that it is mainly the variable cost, forms the core of revenue expenditure.
- this anticipated expenditure core would seem perfectly compatible with the predicted budget.
- No variation from the target (if properly calculated) would be expected.
- In reality there would be small variations about the target line.

Figure 6.1. Continuous predictable—day-to-day spending

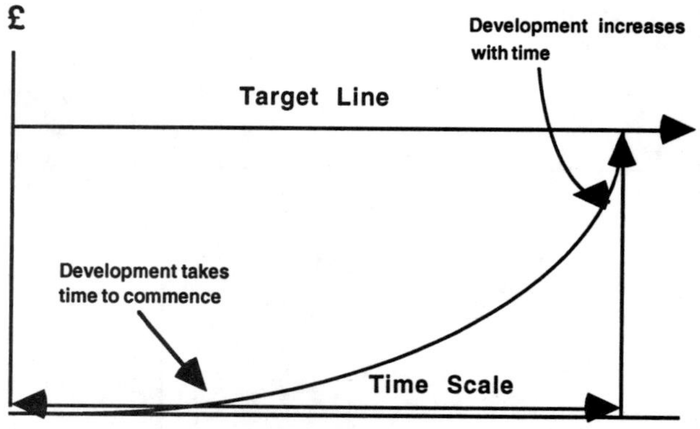

- Development expenditure behaviour is usually associated with new developments including capital spending.
- Characteristics are:
  - spending is not usually apparent until some time after the period has commenced. This is mainly due to the difficulties experienced in stimulating and attracting the required physical resources; and
  - as the period progresses, spending increases rapidly until the target is reached.
- Problems are mainly concerned with managing the project(s) so that targets are reached within the time allocated.
- Retraction is the result of the need to achieve significant savings. The behaviour pattern is the reverse of the illustration above.

Figure 6.2. Development/retraction mode

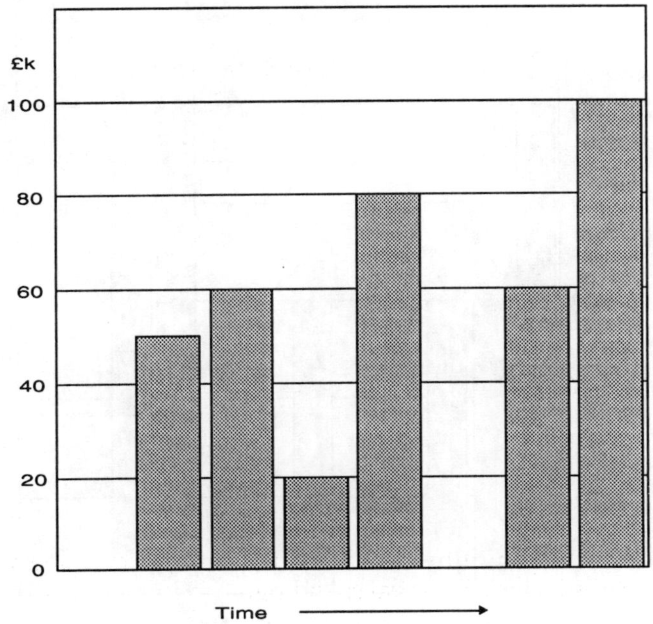

- In this category budgets are demand responsive, special purpose and other frequent charges.
- The allocation of both time and money are specific, but activity within the defined limits may fluctuate.
- It can range from a continuous flow of expenditure, through an erratic performance, to an all at once commitment which could happen at any juncture within the time frame.
- Examples of these kinds of budgets are holiday or sickness relief staff, and some training budgets.
- Minor replacements of plant, machinery, furniture and equipment, and some repair budgets may also occur.
- Although the expected expenditure appears haphazard it would be unusual for the total money made available to be exceeded.

Figure 6.3. Casual expenditure

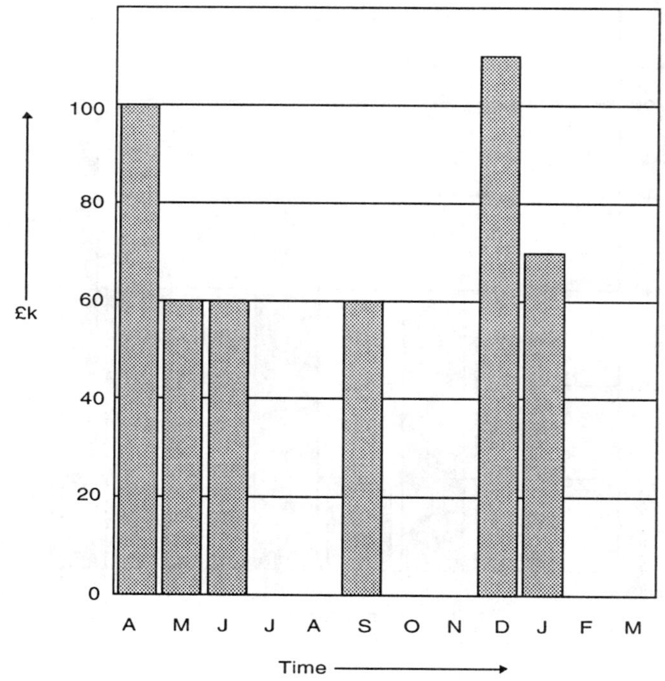

Extra bank holiday payments

- This category includes charges which are fixed and known.
- These type of charges occur at irregular intervals.
- They cover surges in expenditure at defined intervals such as bank holidays or holiday pay.
- Available funds may be allocated separately to each incident or disbursed on specific occasions.
- Extra bank holiday payments might have an impact as displayed above.

Figure 6.4. Infrequent predictable

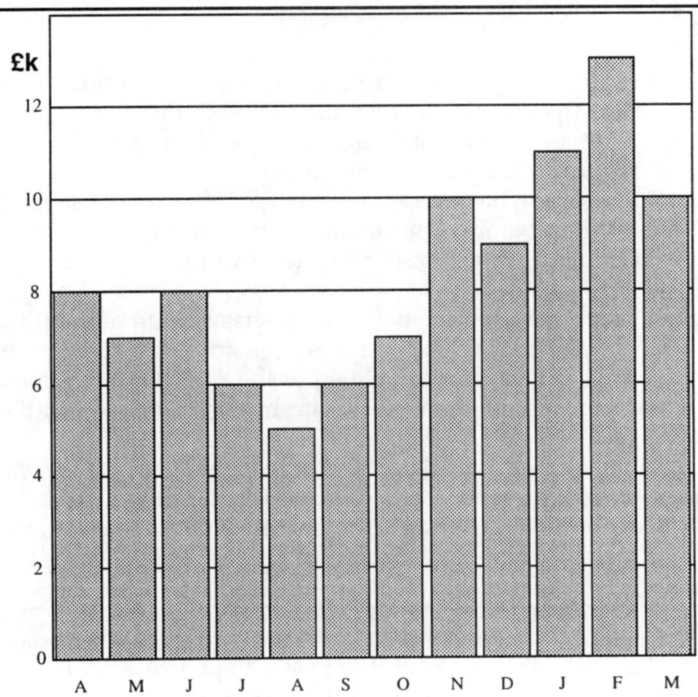

Profiled heating budget

- These are appropriate where there is a distinct but gradual variation according to seasonal or other influences.
- A good example would be the cost of heating, which obviously varies, or should vary, in response to outside air temperature.
- Expenditure would follow this pattern and would tend to be higher in winter than in summer.

Figure 6.5. Profiled budgets

Inflation

In more recent times, the government has attempted to control inflation by imposing cash limits upon both pay awards and price increases. This has meant that where pay negotiators have made agreements which exceeded the limit set, the deficit must be recouped by budget managers.

In addition, the recession has caused a reduction in turnover rates. Staff tend to stay longer in post than before. The financial effect of this phenomenon is that particularly salaried staff, in general terms, tend to move further up the incremental scale.

This so-called 'incremental drift' both diminishes resource mobility and is an additional financial burden which has a direct impact upon budget holders whose salary budgets are usually calculated at the mid point of scales. As far as price increases are concerned, again these are not often funded to the expected level.

When an amount has been calculated and agreed, elements of this can be introduced as the year progresses in accordance with the prices are said to move. Another way is to add into the budget increments which are one-seventy-eighth of the total price increase money available (see Table 6.1).

Month	Increment	Cumulative totals	Month (cont.)	Increment (cont.)	Cumulative totals
April	1	1	October	7	28
May	2	3	November	8	36
June	3	6	December	9	45
July	4	10	January	10	55
August	5	15	February	11	66
September	6	21	March	12	78

Table 6.1. Budget increments

The structure of the total contract price will therefore alter as the year progresses.

Key points summary

- **Ensure that the contract implementation plan is properly reflected in the budget detail.**
- **Budget contract conditions in most organisations can seldom be found in one document.**
- **Performance measures usually take the form of a collection of reports.**
- **It is important that budget managers ensure that all relevant information is accessible to them.**
- **Delays and difficulties can cause interruption.**
- **Budget managers must therefore ensure that minimum contract data sets come regularly into their possession so that their activities can be justified and intervention outcomes assessed and reviewed.**
- **Budget contract income and budget allocations must be made to coincide with the time frame.**
- **Budget managers must ensure that their budgets are allocated according to the source of income.**
- **They must ensure that their budgets are split in parallel with the task to be performed.**
- **Budgets should be profiled according to the expected expenditure behaviour pattern.**

Note

- **In the checklist to Chapters 5 and 6, contract conditions are reconciled with budgetary expectation.**
- **However, the purpose of working through the checklist is to avoid the retraction option by a constant process of reviewing and finding new sources of income.**
- **The checklist is not exhaustive but should stimulate the budget manager to keep sources of income constantly under review.**
- **This is an important and valid method of solving budget problem.**

After reading Chapters 5 and 6

Checklist on budget contract income and budget profiles

- Make sure budget allocations reflect the correct mode (see Figure 6.6)

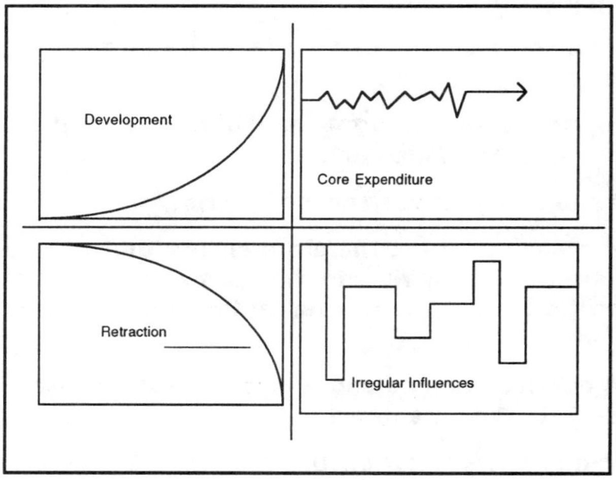

Figure 6.6. Performance modes

- Establish that each mode attracts income in its own right.
- Examine the day-to-day allocation (core spending) carefully to see whether any feature could be included in any of the other patterns—there may be money available where this is so.
- When satisfied that each mode correctly reflects the performance expected look at all the possible income sources from which benefit might be derived (see Figure 6.7).

Type of spending mode	Possible source of additional income
Development	• Capital monies, non-recurring revenue; new revenue monies, internal savings reallocated. • Free funds. • Other funding arrangements.
Retraction	• Bridging finance.
Core spending	• Main contract sources, quasi trading activities. • Reallocated savings. • Free funds.
Erratic influences	• Reallocate and reprofile.

Figure 6.7. Income sources

Case study

An in-house catering contract had a total value of £996,017 for the operating year. Under the contract, uplifts are allowed for inflation and any other variations in the service which are mutually agreed. During the year, price increases of £15,000 and pay awards amounting to £42,000 were agreed. The pay awards were finally paid in the 38th week: the contracted figures for Weeks 37, 38, and 39 are shown in Table 6.2.

Detail	Target for year £	Target for Week 37 £	Target for Week 38 £	Target for Week 39 £
Predictable demand	895,693	17,225	17,225	17,225
Unpredictable demand	50,098	100	205	9,902
Bank holidays	29,705			
Relief staff	20,521			2,007
Basic contract price	**996,017**	**17,325**	**17,430**	**29,134**
Pay awards	12,000		800	800
Arrears	30,000		30,000	
Prices	15,000	519	519	519
New services	30,000	577	577	577
Adjusted contract price	**1,083,017**	**18,421**	**49,326**	**31,030**
Add other income	368,000	7,077	7,077	7,077
Final allocations	**1,451,017**	**25,498**	**56,403**	**38,107**

Table 6.2. Annual and weekly pay awards

The effects of these routine variations together with other agreed additions cause considerable differences in the profiles of the weeks that are affected. If the final allocation for the year had simply been divided by 55 the budgeted portion would be £27.9k. This would have produced quite different results from the profiles shown in Table 6.2. Figure 6.8 illustrates these differences.

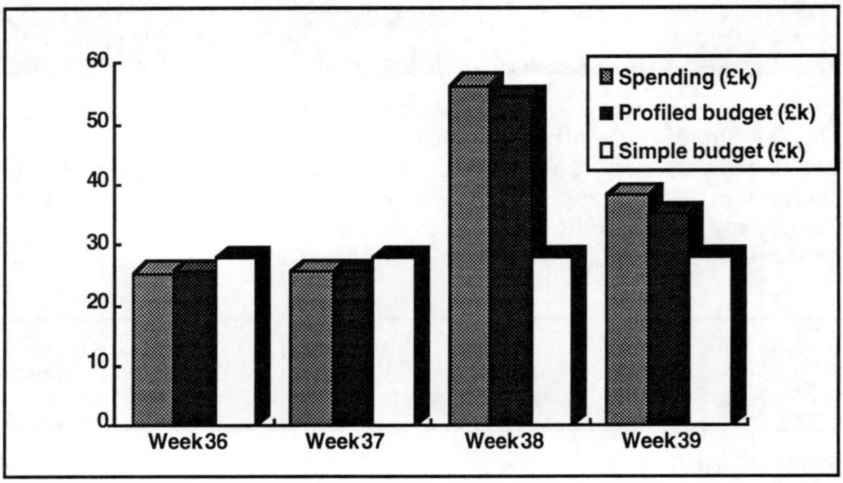

Figure 6.8. Variations in budget calculations

7

Monitoring a budget

Objectives

The purpose of this chapter is to demonstrate that the budget monitoring process extends beyond the passive activity of observing and analysing budget progress. It embraces a much comprehensive approach. Monitoring emphasises a systematic approach. It provides a bridge which links planning, profiling and setting a budget to the potential need to intervene and gain control of a particular position. Specifically:

- It concentrates upon the origin and development of a budgetary need:
  - the complex nature of pipeline commitments;
  - decisions about priority spending;
  - factors which influence them; and
  - how decision packages are made up.
- Rationalising decision packages relating to priority spending it establishes the need to track the progress of a commitment to spend.
- This track is followed from the demand signal through the supply chain, to the fulfilment of the outstanding commitment.

Introduction to commitment management

When a spending direction has been established, tasks are divided, budgets planned and profiled and targets for a particular period set. In order to comply with these objectives, it is necessary to create a process which both ensures their achievement and rationally measures progress towards that achievement. The monitoring process consistently compares progress with the plan, detects deviations from that plan and signals the need to intervene.

In examining income and expenditure trends, it might be supposed that these may be influenced and managed within the limits of money and time. It has to be recognised, however, that expenditure, while it represents the final effect of financial decision taking and is, in that context, historical, is not therefore, in itself, amenable to change. It is an accurate record of the accumulated results of financial activity within that relevant time-frame and in consequence, will be the acid test of the adequacy of management intervention.

When, in the final analysis these trends and patterns are compared with the target, two important facets, the corporate plan, and the ability to manage control within the plan cannot be ignored. In moving away from a purely historical record-keeping situation and towards a better financially managed environment we enter a realm of predictions, inhibitions and aspirations which requires more information than is bestowed through permutations of cash, debtors, creditors, stocks, etc.

This movement from passive record keeping to more active participation, intervention and regulation does not signify a rejection either of historical record or of obligation. Indeed, the implications of past decisions have as important a bearing on current opportunities as has previous experience.

Sometimes the combined effect of built-in obsolescence, poor financial foresight and long-term implications of cash ebb and flow threaten the validity of cash flow planning and may characterise an imminent catastrophe. In the micro system, although working within delegated authority, managers may implement a spending activity on expertise, or goods and services at infrequent and perhaps unfortunate intervals so that the matching of income and expenditure has a haphazard and at best fortuitous appearance.

The budget manager receives an allocation of time and money but, clearly, account has also to be taken of both the agreed plan and the opportunities for control. Although these resources should represent a certain level of purchasing power, because of marginal activity it is unlikely that this strict relationship will be maintained. The budget manager must inevitably have regard to this situation and through it, attempt control. It is therefore at this juncture that control is gained or lost. The ability to systematically monitor a situation is therefore a key competence.

Developing the approach

Perhaps the most challenging aspect of developing this monitoring feature is the rationalisation of decision packages within the money time framework. Although these packages, by their very nature, will in the interim exceed resources available, they must in the final analysis be made to equal expenditure and budget. This is illustrated in Figure 7.1.

- B is taken to represent the total budget available;
- E is expenditure; and
- C is the outstanding commitment.

During the financial period, commitment to expenditure will be greater than actual expenditure. Indeed, commitment may at times be greater than the budget available but, through the management process this is controlled within the time limit.

Two situations, illustrated in Table 7.1 and Figure 7.2 can be expressed. The first applies at any time during the time-frame and the second is at its termination:

1. Where time limit has not expired: $\{B - (E + C)\} < 0$.
2. At the end of the period when the objectives have been met and the time limit has expired:

$$B = E \text{ and}$$
$$C = 0.$$

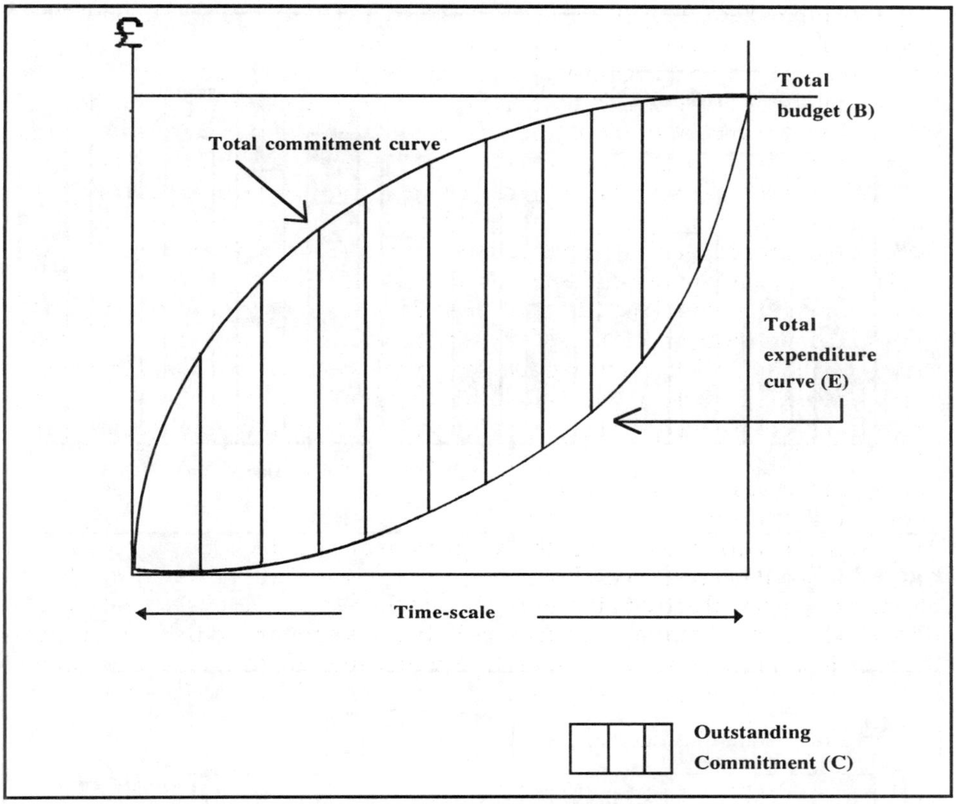

Figure 7.1. The basic commitment model

Cumulatives (£k)	Apr	May	Jne	Jly	Aug	Sept	Oct	Nov	Dec	Jan	Feb	Mar
Spending E	8.0	16.5	24.8	34	43	53	63.5	74.0	84.5	95	107	120
O/s commitment C	21.7	32.2	40.2	35	32	29	26.0	22.5	23.0	15	5	0
Total commitment	29.7	48.7	65.0	69	75	82	89.5	96.5	107.5	110	110	120

Table 7.1. A well managed commitment

Table 7.1 shows a well managed commitment which at no time is allowed to exceed the budget of £120k. Although the expenditure does not occur in equal increments, (£10k each month) the budget manager has made sure that outstanding commitments were maintained at a level which adequately controlled spending throughout the period.

A third situation can occur both during and at the end of a financial period when commitment exceeds the budget. The time limit has not expired but commitment already exceeded the budget:

$$\{B - (E + C)\} < 0 \quad [\text{where } E < B].$$

This is illustrated in Figure 7.3.

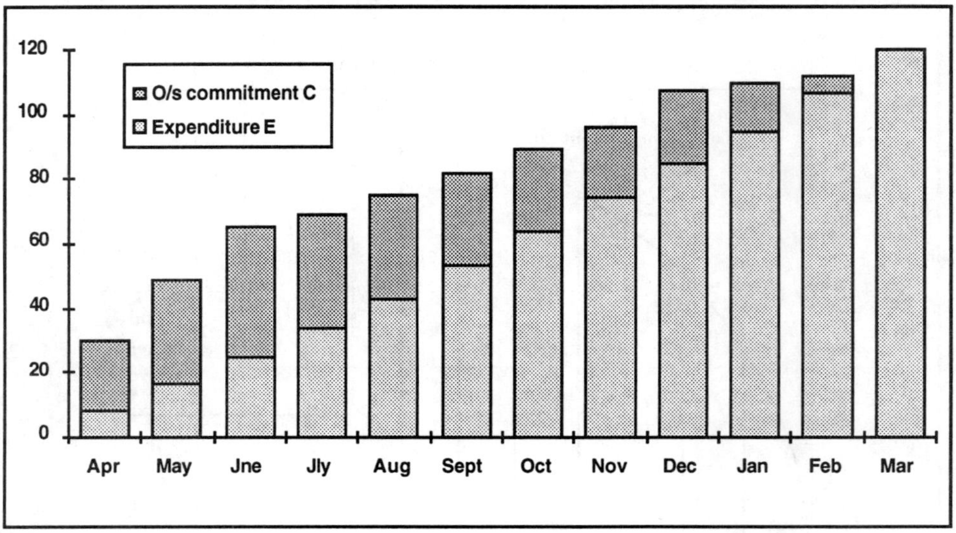

Figure 7.2. Commitment example

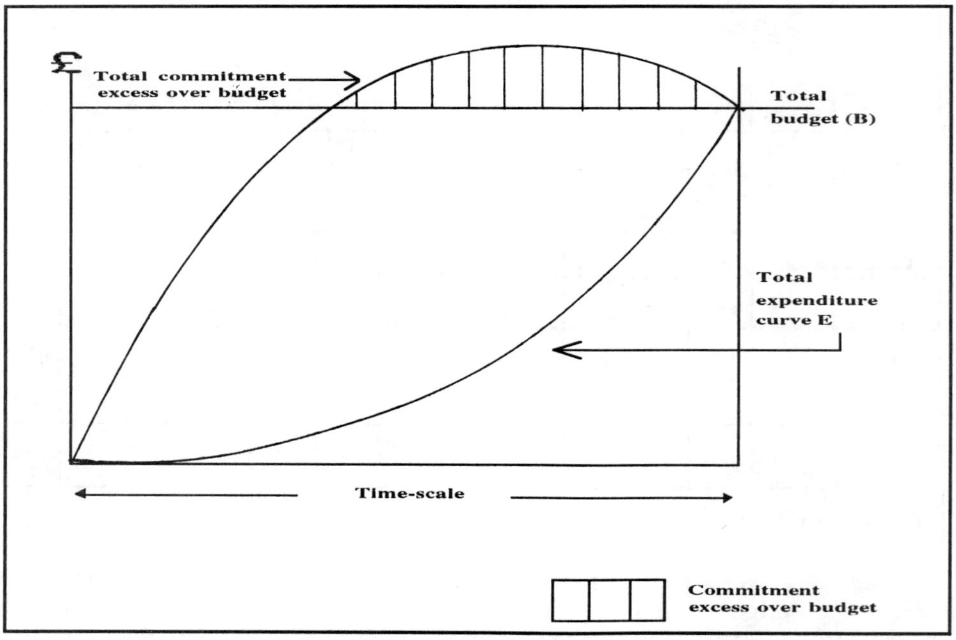

Figure 7.3. Extending the commitment model

Thus rather than considering the variation position, emphasis is placed on the balance remaining. The outstanding commitment and the balance of the budget are the two factors that regulate decision taking.

Having regard to the time-scale, budget management centres on a constant review of outstanding commitment in the context of current delivery pattern.

Towards the end of the period, the position will be modified by extracting commitments which are unlikely to come to fruition in time and other more promising items substituted, the original schemes becoming, where appropriate, a commitment in the new period.

Tracking

In order to gain control of the spending cycle it is necessary to keep a record of the various stages through which a financial episode will pass. It is also important that budgets are managed in such a way that controlled events which can

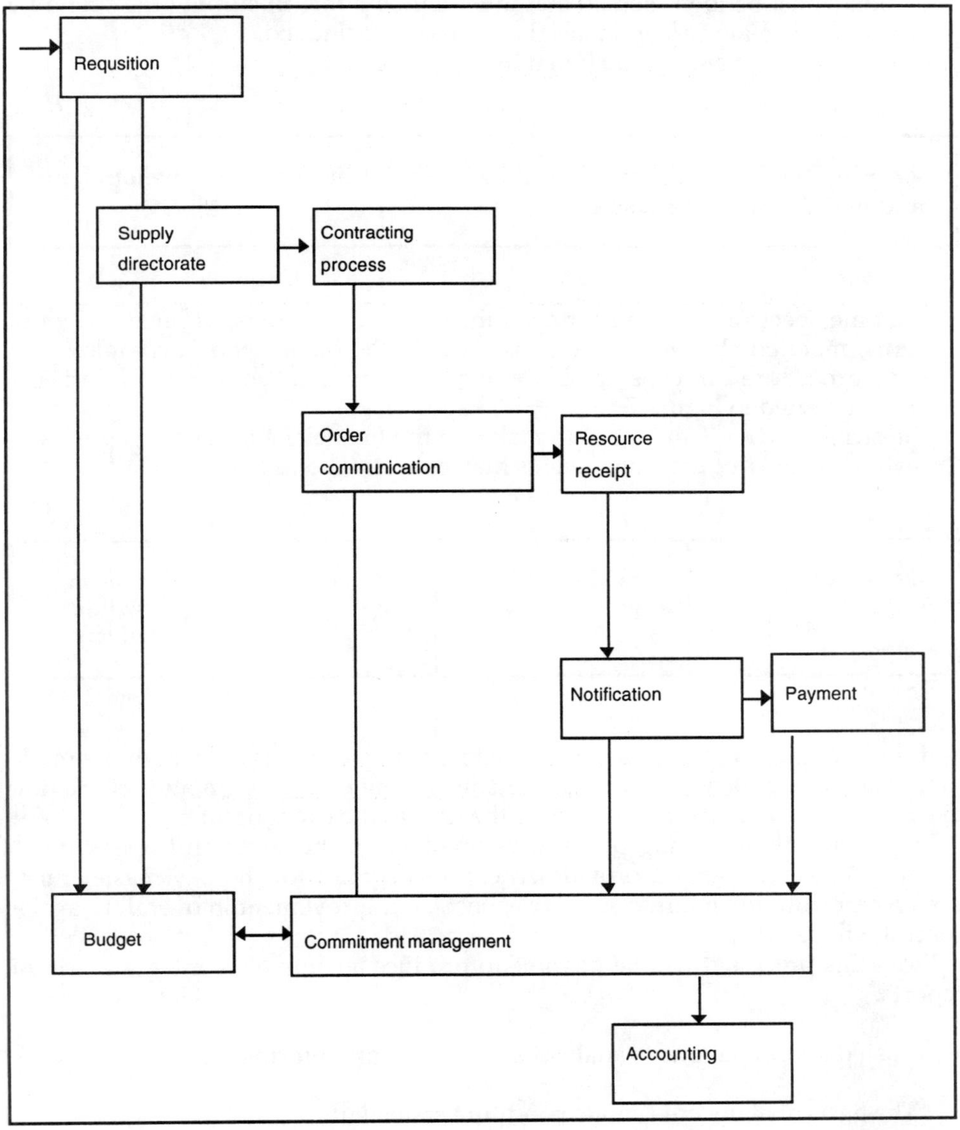

Figure 7.4. Financial events trail

result from an inability to plan are reduced to manageable proportions. This means that assets which are nearing the end of their useful and cost-effective life are identified in sufficient time to plan for their replacement or redeployment. Through this process the budget manager is placed in a more competent position from which to judge how best financial resources may be allocated during a particular financial period. The advent of a financial episode can therefore be predicted at a specific time and place and the budget set accordingly.

Provided that existing resources are subjected to the management process, their need for replacement can be generally signalled through the production of a requisition. This will commence the commitment cascade which should terminate with the fulfilment of the objectives. The progress of the episode must be tracked throughout so that comparison with the budget is possible. Significant deviations must be identified so that intervention either in curbing the spending programme or re-allocating financial resources is facilitated.

A trail of these events is illustrated in Figure 7.4.

Keeping track of these events can be managed through the development and maintenance of records.

The time spectrum can be shortened through repeat orders, unreviewed work patterns, metered changes, or stock issues. On the other hand, a complex purchasing procedure can considerably elongate the time taken to fulfil a decision. This is illustrated in Figure 7.5.

The string of events that goes to make up the financial episode is lengthy and the events varied but the major events may be identified as being:

Decision stage	→	**Commitment stage**	→	**Fulfilment**	→	**Payment creditor/ delivery**

and the content of the events diary may be as simple as this or it might be made more elaborate depending on requirements. In any case, it is a matter of moving the value of the item from one stage to the next as the event occurs.

In addition the checking procedures involved in the successful operation of commitment management provide an extra safeguard for the pay master function. Apart from the internal security aspect, an improvement in overall financial control will be noted.

From this process it will be possible to produce a completely integrated set of reports:

- Cash disposal payments analysis and event diary information.
- The basis of an income and expenditure statement.
- Comprehensive commitment management information.

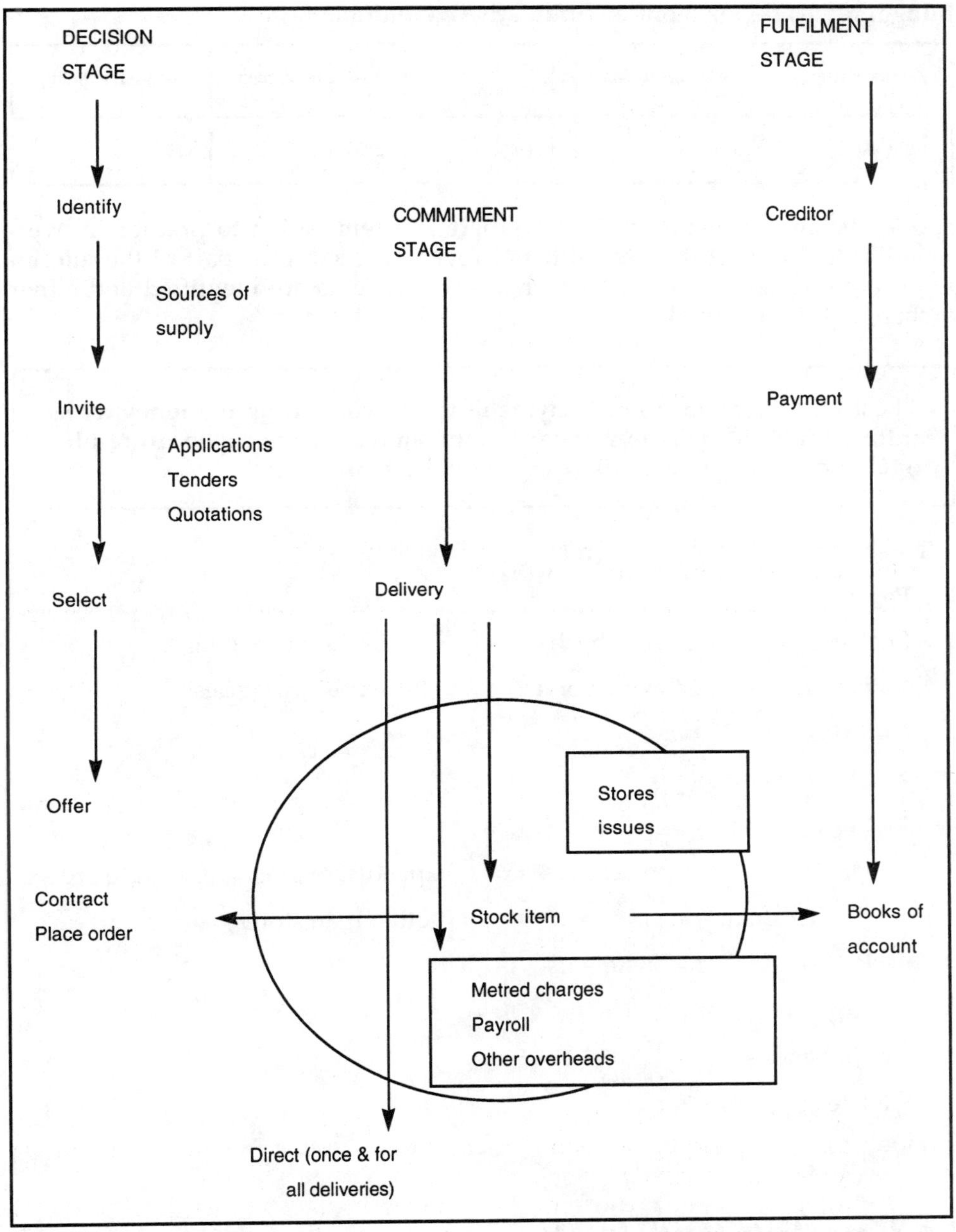

Figure 7.5. The commitment completion

Commitment management application

In identifying an event before it has time to have an expenditure impact, the fundamental change in the emphasis of reporting tends to confuse the uninitiated. The budget report which will no longer have a variation factor will look something like:

Budget report for six months' cumulative commitment

Annual budget	Expenditure to date	Outstanding commitment	Total commitment	Balance remaining
£120,000	£53,000	£29,000	£82,000	£39,000

and as 'balance remaining' declines there is a temptation to predict an over-spending position. It is essential that a review procedure is part of the interim reporting mechanism so that marginal commitments are identified and either exchanged or eliminated.

The accuracy of the system may be tested by comparing in money terms information gleaned from independent sources. Thus expenditure plus outstanding commitment is equal to total commitment.

Total commitment components:

1. **Payroll**

   Realistic commitment established = Expenditure plus
   Valuation (provided by personnel) agreed vacancies

2. **Non-payroll**
   - Direct payments)
   - Stores issues)
   - Order for items and services = Expenditure plus outstanding orders
     (* other than stores) (* other than stores)
   - Price and other adjustments)
   - Any other contractual)
     obligations

   * delete as appropriate

Payroll components

Although the recruitment and employment of staff is sometimes regarded as the purchase of expertise, it is not strictly speaking compatible with the acquisition of other assets because of its transient nature.

Within certain limitations, employment contracts may be terminated on either side and this produces a theoretical flexibility which is not so apparent with other purchases. On the other hand, perpetual payroll commitment differs from an outright purchase in that the latter does not usually generate the same direct financial consequences. Employment flexibility may therefore be contrasted against both the ongoing financial burden and complete ownership: it might be concluded that a wage or salary is more like rental payments rather than a permanent acquisition expenditure.

In many ways, however, it would be unfortunate to regard a workforce as 'rented'. Collectively it would be regarded as more permanent than such terminology would suggest. Indeed it could be argued that an organisation, while not owning a workforce or its expertise, does actually purchase more intangible assets such as goodwill and loyalty. Whatever view is taken, it is clear that there is a distinction between the flexibility inherent in the employment of an individual and the general attitude towards the total workforce.

Attitudes to employment problems, which affect these intangible assets, are in themselves costly and certain indicators are therefore worthy of regular scrutiny.

Managing vacancy stock provides employment for the personnel department and increases opportunities for better budgetary management but may also be a financial burden because of its very existence.

Moving on then to recruitment, here too, selection procedures can be unduly costly both in limiting the market and in bureaucracy. In addition, staffing structure frequently generates, through grievance mechanisms, unexpected spending.

These three vital areas contribute to hitherto unrecognised financial burdens which, though they will be contained within overall budgets, are not specifically costed. While these are all aspects of a normal personnel policy, and are part of a continuous activity, it is nevertheless desirable, to ensure that incidents should be minimised.

The relationship between flexibility of individual employment and the continuous nature of total payroll commitment is partially expressed in:

Current payroll cost plus cost of current terminations (potential future vacancies)
equals
cost of potential total commitment

Where vacancies to be filled equal terminations then payroll costs will always equal potential commitment. Where vacancies or terminations become significant, then recruitment and employment procedures may themselves be contributory factors to an escalating phenomenon. When large numbers are recruited or discharged, financial consequences can result both from the activity itself and from the procedure.

Other spending components

At times it might be felt that there was a certain relentless pressure on funds, yet the case of goods and services is in many ways more flexible, particularly in respect of the acquisition, repair or replacement of assets. Here, unlike payroll, purchasing can be initiated, continued or discounted more or less as the situation requires. Having already dealt with orders for direct delivery, there are also commitments for which no orders are placed or where deliveries are made to a central store.

A system of direct payment is usually employed to cope with such items as rent, insurance, service contracts and metered charges like telephones, electricity, gas, water, etc. These payments are often made in a haphazard way which from a financial point of view will be made more consistent through creditor or advance payment adjustments. An example of this type of problem and is solution is shown in Table 7.2.

Contract	Incidental contract detail	For period	Amount for that period	Fixed commitment for year	Possible variation	TOTAL
Lift service		3-monthly payment	379	1,516		1,516
	incidentals:					
	extra labour		135			
	extra expenses		27		800	800
	extra materials		32			
Rentals						
Telephone		3 month	45	180		180
	incidentals:					
	calls		122		440	440
Other fixed charge		full year	919	919		919
Metered charges						
Electricity						
	(standing)		13		1,690	1,690
	(metered)		511			
			2,183	**2,615**	**2,930**	**5,545**

Table 7.2. Direct payment

Approaching the problem with commitment techniques, all fixed charge elements are known for the year and the commitment can be easily calculated. It would, of course, be foolish to strike a budget which does not coincide with the estimate unless some political (in the parochial sense) point is being made. Metered or other elements are amenable to various treatments ranging from additions to existing commitments as they occur, to the assumption that the target has already been reached and any variation to expectation is adjusted on this maximum.

Key points summary

- **Commitment management is an active rather than a passive method of monitoring budget performance.**
- **It takes account of current expenditure and any other item that the budget manager has requested.**
- **The methodology is sophisticated and can be applied to any form of expenditure.**
- **Keeping a record and a dairy of events is not difficult.**
- **Commitment management is based on the theory that the balance remaining in a budget after deducting all those items which will during the financial period be charged to it can be effectively managed so that spending and budget totals are made to coincide at the end of the period.**
- **Where, at any time, during a financial period, commitments are in danger of exceeding the budget, contracts must be either deferred to a more acceptable time or cancelled.**

Case study

In order to balance the financial plan for the new financial year, the Treasurer had to find a reliable source that would yield additional savings.

Despite 'X' previous problems, 'X' appeared to have managed a consistent underspending in the current year. 'X' had ended up with a total underspending of £100k in a budget of £2.5m. The Treasurer decided that 'X' could afford to make a bigger contribution on the basis of a more equitable distribution of funds. 'X' argued that stock of vacant posts had been reduced (partly due to retraction). 'X' needed to fill some existing vacancies to improve safety standards.

The reduction the Treasurer now proposed would simply result in an overspending in the new year. 'X' produced a table to illustrate the situation (see Table 7.3).

Cumulatives (£m)	Apr	May	Jne	Jly	Aug	Sept	Oct	Nov	Dec	Jan	Feb	Mar
Spending	0.21	0.41	0.62	0.81	0.98	1.19	1.39	1.58	1.81	2.01	2.19	2.39
Vacancy cost	0	0.01	0.01	0.02	0.06	0.06	0.07	0.80	0.07	0.07	0.10	0.11

Table 7.3. Overspending chart

'X' said at the end of the year the vacancy stock was valued at £110k or ten whole-time equivalent staff. 'X' had already interviewed and issued contracts to fill 12 posts (this included two terminations which had occurred in February and were not included in the above figures).

The Treasurer regretted that the decision regarding redistribution of resources had now been taken and 'X' would have to compensate for this excess through natural wastage.

8

Tactical intervention

Objectives

- It has already been seen that stategic intervention in the direction of spending is part of the business planning and other methodologies discussed in Part 1.
- Intervention is the tool used to implement a financial plan but it may also be used on a much smaller scale to make minor corrections.
- The purpose of this chapter is to show how interventionist techniques can be most effectively applied at a tactical or operational level in order to ensure compliance with contract management and general good house-keeping.
- Intervention is usually required in order to change an expenditure pattern to some more desirable outcome.
- In practice, it is important that the budget manager can analyse a situation in order to implement the correcting influence.
- Specifically the chapter sets out:

  – the general principles that govern effective intervention;

  – the dependence upon quality of decision taking; and

  – the capacity of a budget manager to react to a particular situation.
- Also considered is a variety of factors likely to impair a manager's capacity to intervene.

General principles

The government's capacity and authority for financial intervention is an important measure which is used to control public expenditure. It is also a device which the government may use to improve economic prospects. An authority may also make use of intervention:

- to redirect expenditure;

- to curb excessive expenditure; or
- as a general modifying influence which will assure the achievement of targets.

As the main burden of any change will almost certainly fall upon budget managers, it is important that they become competent in the execution of intervention. The purposes of their intervention are therefore similar to those listed above.

Spending patterns developed by budget managers may require redirection, reduction or modification.

Normally, where there is no interference with the budget target, a general core of expenditure will proceed as described in Chapters 5 and 6. That is to say there will be minimal fluctuations about the target line except perhaps a tendency to overspend due to the impact of inflation or perhaps lack of resistance to a continual demand for improvement.

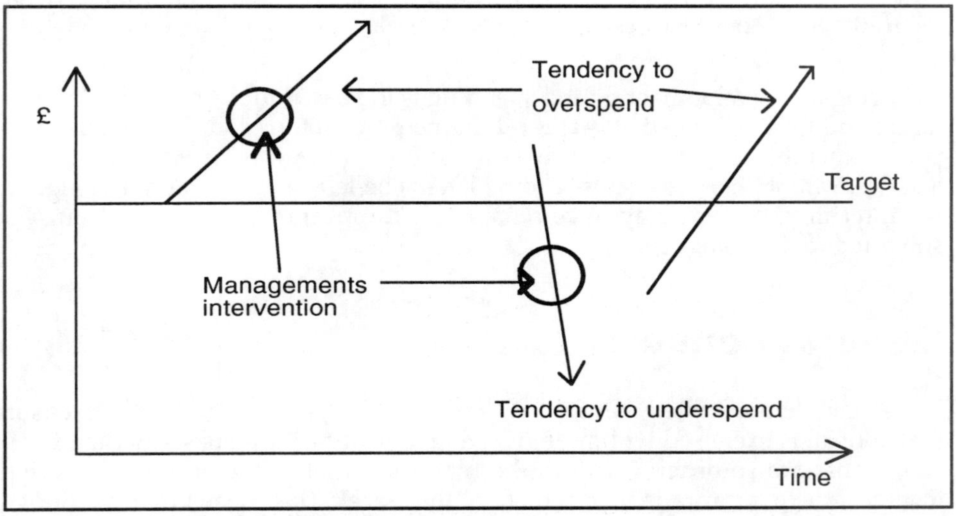

Figure 8.1. Effective intervention

In Figure 8.1 the budget manager has modified activities through minimal intervention so that tendencies to overspend or to underspend are corrected. The net result of this activity can, over time, produce a curve which will have the appearance of a sine wave. This kind of intervention conforms with the description appropriate to a continuous predictable budget.

Where a major change in direction is required, although the budget manager requires to be much more proactive, the effects conform to the pattern already established except that the new budget settlement will be at a higher or lower level than the original. This is illustrated in Figure 8.2.

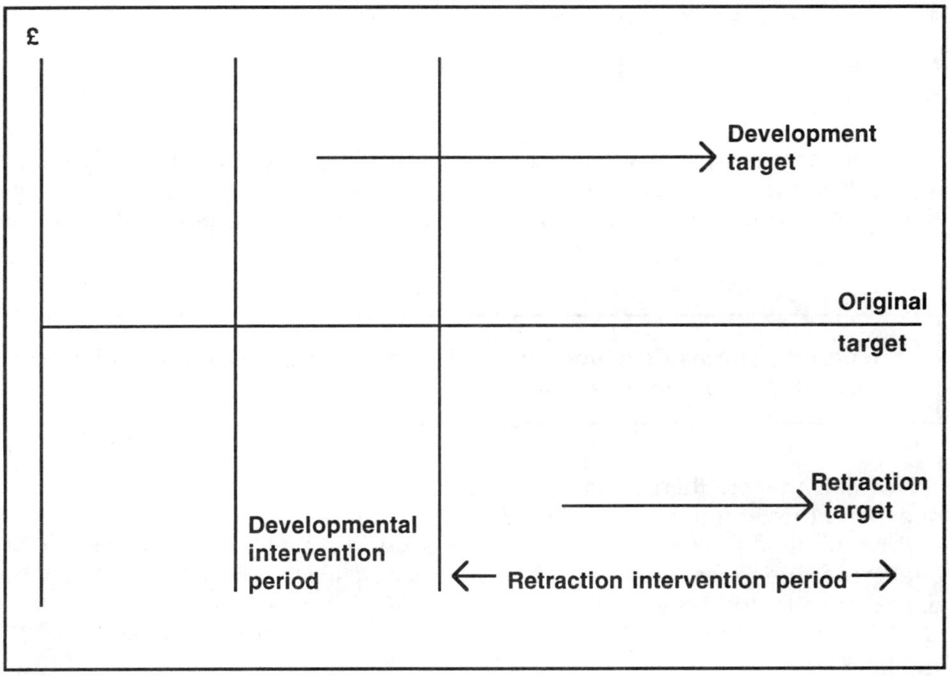

Figure 8.2. Significant changes

During the development period spending is increased to the new development target and later remained at that level. In the retraction period the converse happens. Expenditure is systematically reduced until the new reduced level has been achieved. In neither case can spending events be left to chance and although, in the interim, a pattern may have a haphazard appearance, each event must be subjected to the plan.

General constraints

It has been demonstrated that the key activity in budget management is to ensure that control is exercised within defined and agreed parameters so that the financial events are so ordered within the time limit that at the end of the period, income or expenditure is made to equal the target. This means that the budget manager must be confident that the information given is a true reflection of the management activity being undertaken. For example, if a moratorium has been applied to a particular aspect (say an overtime ban) in order to correct an overspending trend, then the budget manager would expect no further spending in this area. As a result of this action it might be expected that the savings arising would be reallocated. A facility would need to exist which both permitted the transfer or virement to take place and to adequately reflect this in interim reports.

The five main types of budget profiles discussed in Chapter 6:

- continuous predictable;
- development/retraction modes;

- casual expenditure;
- infrequent but predictable expenditure; and
- profiled expenditure;

require different treatment in interim reports so that the activities of a budget manager can be properly interpreted. In this context it should be noted that where more significant intervention is required, the techniques appropriate to these types may be used. Timing (or punctuality as one of the acceptance characteristics) of interim reports have a significant impact upon the scope for management action. This scope can be examined from three view points:

- time delay between the end of the period being reported upon and the time when the report is received;
- time factor involved in implementing a change in the expenditure pattern;
- delay in observing the consequences of management intervention.

These factors all become critical when either the balance of resources remaining in a budget increasingly diminishes, or towards the end of a financial period when the time limit tends to expire. The principles of resource mobility can be applied where mobility is taken to be all those elements which change or tend to change a state of financial inertia or a rate of resource expenditure.

Although either the balance of resources or the time remaining may limit a manager's opportunities to influence a final outcome in a given period, some negotiating possibilities may still exist where it can be argued that the financial episode extends beyond the period of time under scrutiny.

In general terms, report timing could be said to have the following implications:

- **Initial indication delay** compounds the position by the rate of variation growth divided by the delay.
- **Intervention possibilities** are limited to only those resources which have a balance remaining and which are amenable to timely intervention.

  This is closely connected with the permanency of a particular resource. For example, property management is less amenable than resource allocations which have short life spans, such as overtime and possibly temporary staffing.
- **Intervention observational delays** in a complex budget environment where serial intervention may be prevalent, observation of the financial effects requires considerable analysis. Delay in producing interim reports may therefore further confuse the issues involved.

For example, factors such as overtime, on call, extra duty payments, natural wastage and the level of temporary staffing are amenable to modification. Theoretically, it would be possible to curb some of these and to cease some practices.

Case study

In Table 8.1 a range of variations are shown against different locations within the catering contract budget.

Budget Manager's Name: Mrs O'Nyons Catering contract
Cumulative payroll budget for 3-month period April–June 1994

Location	Budget £	Spend £	+/- £	Staff in post	Average cost
A	6,207	5,421	-786	3.00	7,228
B	14,581	19,709	5,128	9.50	8,300
C	96,139	107,911	11,772	45.19	9,552
D	9,650	9,427	-223	3.80	9,923
E	2,429	2,282	-147	1.00	9,128
F	6,407	5,912	-495	2.00	11,824
TOTALS	135,413	150,662	15,249	64.49	9,345

Table 8.1. Variations within the catering contract at different locations

Staff Detail and average costs for each location are given in Table 8.2.

Location	Budget £	Staff number	Average cost £
A	24,824	3.00	8,275
B	56,950	7.00	8,136
C	375,570	43.17	8,700
D	37,665	3.81	9,886
E	8,540	1.00	8,540
F	24,984	2.00	12,492
TOTALS	528,533	59.98	8,812

Table 8.2. Staffing and average costs by location

Although no skill mixes or supplementary information has been given here, it is evident from the average costs that a range of grades are spread over the various locations, also the incidence of overtime, absenteeism, etc, may pervert the costs and the budget holder would therefore require access to considerably more information than that which has been provided.

Assuming that the interim report for the first three months of the financial year, ie April to June was not available until some time toward the end of July, the results of significant intervention would not be observed until after the end of August and possibly September.

This could mean that an underlying tendency to overspend could be as high as £30k by the end of September and with only between six or seven

Case study—contd.

months to the end of the financial period, implies the intervention of a progressively more austere nature in order to bring the budget into balance. In effect, by the end of September four to five whole-time equivalent temporary staff would have to be released whereas at the end of June, better management of overtime, etc, might have sufficed.

Observation of the effects of this intervention may also suffer from delay and further measures may have to be taken.

On the other hand, in this case, the budget manager, may already have taken intervention measures and these results (the three months report) may in fact be observational in characteristic. For example, the *funded* establishment is 59.98 yet at the end of June the *actual* whole-time equivalent was 64.49 of which 16.51 were temporary staffing. It is conceivable that an increase of 4.51 in total terms would be permitted *unless* either:

- increased funding was to be made available; or
- extra staffing has been tolerated in order to cope with a short-term work-load peak. In this case the budget could sustain the additional staffing until October/ November when all temporary posts would have to be vacated.

It is apparent, however, that in both these so-called 'permitted' cases the overall interim statement does not reflect the true financial position:

- In the first case additional funding has not been added; and
- in the second, the budget profile has not been sufficiently adjusted.

Budget system acceptability would not therefore comply with a reasonable veracity standard unless some memorial was added by way of explanation. Such a memorial would have to take the line that the system was incapable of accepting the necessary adjustments and credit was extended in some other fashion.

Quality decisions

Accounting periods impose their own limits on available funds but the passage of time is expressed in such terms as production deadlines and delivery dates; turnover ratios also have budgetary consequences which suggest that time as a resource may be sometimes disposed of by expediency.

As with other factors of production, a temptation exists to expedite a request in the exchange situation as a result of the expiring time limit or to offer a modest alternative because of a lack of funds. Expediency would never be viewed as an efficient device and for this reason most organisations ensure that some sort of administrative machinery is available to frustrate potentially wasteful endeavours. This in turn creates a dilemma in the response to urgency, which is tempered by natural caution (see Figure 8.3).

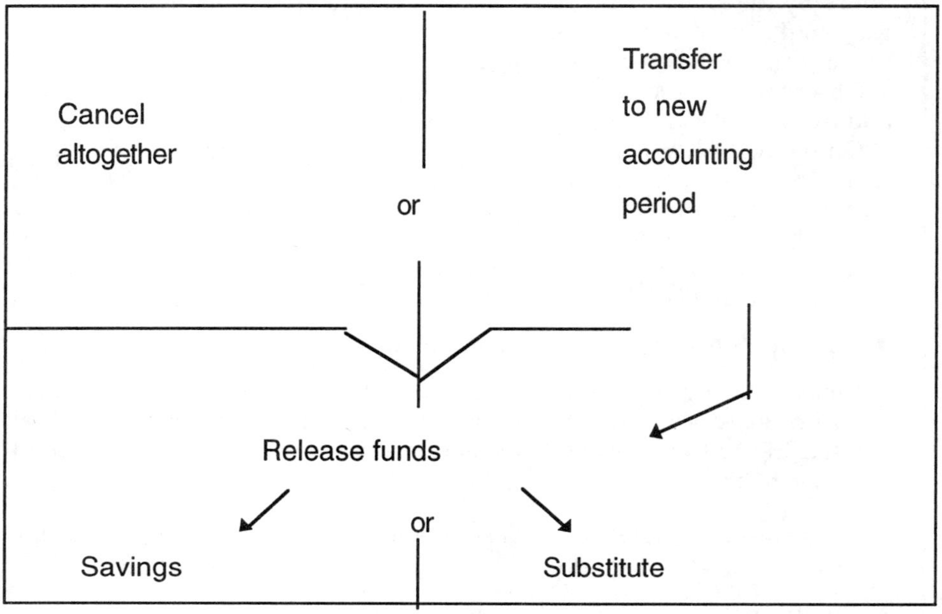

Figure 8.3. Exchange dilemma

In many cases, where the comparative balances indicate a substantial overspending, it is apparent that budgetary episodes encompass a much longer time span than the neat time frame into which resources are finally allocated. Indeed, it might be argued that an episode is never really complete but some characteristics emerge which identify a variety of episodes which may be equated with the time-frames already discussed. The main distinguishing feature depends, however, on the resolution of the expediency/caution dilemma.

The 'expedient' situation, where the consultative machinery has been only partially adopted or totally ignored, can result only in dissatisfaction and is the acid test of quality. During the early stages, changes in system would be necessary to eliminate the possibility that either too much frustration is caused through cumbersome systems based on a cautionary approach or too much dissatisfaction arises through the expedient.

Yet, having identified a genuine need, and having perceived a business opportunity which will support that need, the ability of an organisation to dispose of funds within the limits is a measure of its progressive image. Therefore, in satisfying management's acquisitive nature, inherent in the tendency towards organised purchase, there should be no apparent loss of momentum, yet, the sequence of events may envisage a fairly long consultative process which might involve a number of groups of interested parties.

In the multidisciplinary environment the sanctity of delegated authority and speed in decision taking is inhibited both by good purchasing practice and by the need to consult. On the other hand, in making good use of a range of expertise in the corporate context, the logical progression of events may be so organised that needs and opportunities are so graded that a scale of priorities is established prior to the budgetary period.

The source of the perceived needs may not always originate only in the mind's eye of the budget holder but most organisations rely on automatic asset review. In this case it is desirable to extend beyond the compass of the asset register to cover all assets, including payroll.

This would follow the following process:

1. Expected working life of all assets including labour are tested against maintenance costs and a timetable of replacement needs. The lifespan of items, goods, services and materials can be fairly accurately assessed and although usually having long-term implications, payroll, too, has obvious and known working life implications. This lifespan inventory can be reviewed in the light of current developments, repairs, sickness, etc, to see whether obsolescence is more inherent.

2. Possible replacement problems are considered against opportunity, alternatives and the potential contribution of the expenditure item to the production pattern. In other words, if it is decided to confirm the asset review findings and to process a firm proposal there should be a clearly defined financial benefit.

3. In conferring the status of a proposal on that which had previously existed merely as a perceived need movement in the decision taking process is implied from one level of a management to another. It would, however, be an intolerable burden and a departure from the concept of delegation to act in this way. Day-to-day expenses such as withdrawals from stock piles or stores and ongoing payroll would not usually be the subject of this kind of review.

   It is intended only to apply to marginal activity where impending obsolescence is detected.

4. When the need has been identified, interested parties consulted, and a proposal framed, further progress can only be made against a background of agreed policy. This usually means that because of limited funds some low-priority items on the shopping list will not be processed but will be kept pending further developments.

5. The episode will continue through commitment and spending in accordance with the outline in Chapter 7, but it is also clear that a twilight episode will also exist for those proposals which were not processed. As time progresses these twilight items may be overtaken by events which establish new priorities and which, together with the original proposals, will form the basis of future episodes.

Effective commitment management, if it had been applied to the example given, would have controlled cash spending during the financial year so that the organisation would have 'lived' within resources available thus eliminating the reduction in asset balances. In addition, the growth in creditors would have been curbed. Overall, the organisation would not have drifted into an overspent position.

Mobility

Resource mobility at any time must be greater than the surplus required. For example, if in financial terms the savings required to balance a budget was S, the resource mobility factor, Rm, should always exceed this (Rm > S). In the balancing situation, as time expires this mobility factor has to proportionately increase. Thus at an expiry time t, S is taken to be constant and the equation can be written:

$$Rmt = S.$$

It follows therefore that where t is very small Rm will become increasingly manageable.

(Where $t \rightarrow o$ $Rm \rightarrow \infty$).

The converse of this also applies. Where, for example, the manager has succeeded in releasing resources and has created a surplus, it may be considered desirable to reallocate this capacity to some developments. The problem in this case would be to introduce a spending requirement which would conform to the same principles. For example, if the corporate budget plan proposes service developments in the order of £3.53m, which is made dependent upon a cost improvement plan of £4.12m, expected resource mobility could be as high as £7.65.

The two aspects, development and retraction, have to be managed in a conterminous way so that an alteration in the balance of service delivery occurs.

This assumes that no transfer of resources between development and improvement is possible, but in effect this is potentially wasteful and usually transfers of resources from one purpose to another would be likely. The main direction of the plan is nevertheless to achieve bottom-line savings of £0.59m and the emerging resource mobility spectrum will therefore lie between £0.59m and £7.65m.

In a climate of change budget managers tend to insure against immobilising factors by creating resource structures which are more flexible. This means that resources which are more amenable are utilised to a greater extent and funding is made available with emphasis on non-recurring items. This reasoning is mainly based upon the expected life span of a particular resource purchase. The stability of an organisation's resource structure is affected in this way.

There is therefore a need to balance flexibility against stability in resource structures so that the organisation itself does not become so mobile that its capacity is damaged or is so stagnant that it can not properly cope with change. Figure 8.4 illustrates the comparisons in the distribution of resource mobility between stable and flexible resource structures in terms of lifespans.

Within the stable model, flexibility is obtained by reducing the potential lifespan of resources. This is achieved through greater dependence on leasing, employment of temporary staff, overtime, etc. Inevitably, as the critical mobility mass is approach, a loss of morale, increases in sickness levels and diminished performance will be observed.

This tendency towards a turbulent as opposed to a dynamic organisation can also be observed in greater staff turnover and a marked unwillingness on the

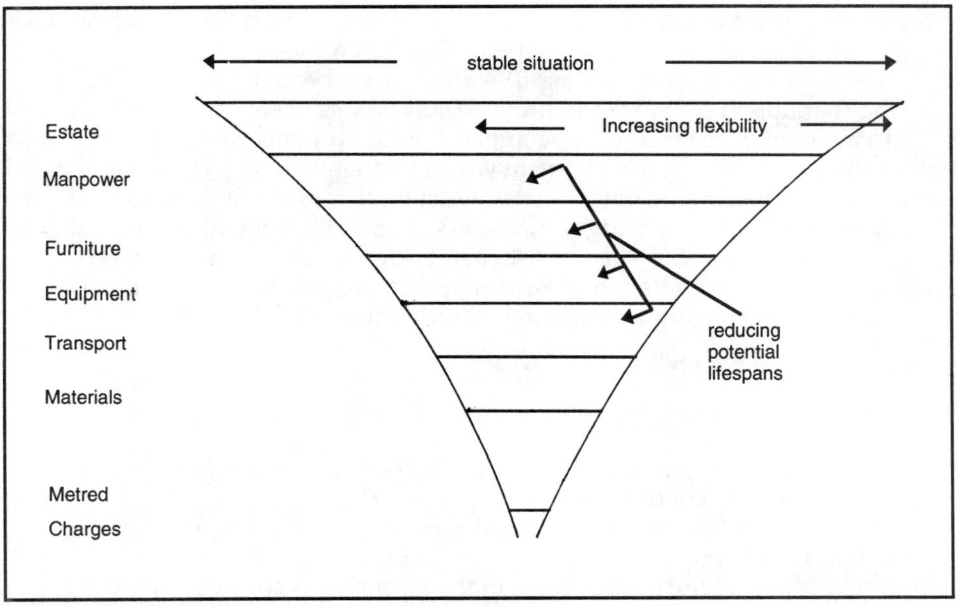

Figure 8.4. Resource structure

part of staff to accept a post within the organisation. It is my own experience that this critical mobility mass often occurs before the final stages of a change can be implemented.

In *Surviving in General Management*[1], I described the financial implications of an alteration in the balance of health care which required the development of a retraction model in acute hospital bed provision with commensurate revenue savings of £0.25m. The central pivot of the model proposed the closure of Skegatilla Hospital to be achieved, in stages, over a six-month period. In order to create the necessary resource mobility, all posts which became vacant through natural wastage, were frozen and only those which were essential were filled on the basis of temporary contracts. Despite considerable union opposition, it became increasingly difficult to maintain staffing levels in the hospital because existing staff were more and more successful in obtaining other posts and prospective candidates for the temporary posts became progressively difficult to find.

In the event, management was able to create a measure of stability through internal redeployment. This was possible because Skegatilla was one of a large hospital group and management therefore had the capacity to cope with a potentially unstable model, but had the situation arisen in a smaller group, then capability to deal with instability would be diminished.

Instability can also occur in customer volumes where it is perceived that a particular facility is likely to be threatened. 'Save our hospital/school . . .' campaigns can themselves be self-fulfilling prophesies where public anxiety about the future of a hospital or school is expressed and at the same time prospective patients, parents or clients may choose to sever traditional links and create new referral patterns which favour a competitor. These campaigns may therefore be cynically viewed by the upper reaches of management whose resolve to rationalise a public service can be enhanced.

Budget managers also have to bear in mind the fact that a long resource life span incurs increasing expenditure by way of running costs and maintenance.

This applies to manpower as well as estate, equipment, transport, etc. These costs also attract a budget and it seems obvious that when these costs exceed the cost of replacement (or are approaching it) consideration would need to be given to invoking that option. However, in order to make a business case, records such as capital valuation register must be compared with an items running, repair and maintenance costs. This infers a system which frequently does not exist and managers may have to compile the case from independent research. It is, however, an important feature which budget managers must comprehend because it will influence senior managers when a particular budget's viability is reviewed.

There are therefore two main pressures upon managers to keep the life span of a particular resource within manageable limits. These are:

- a desire to have mobility;
- the cost of prolonging a lifespan beyond its realistic use

and careful consideration of these factors suggests that there is a need to adequately identify and control them. This implies that budgetary control mechanisms must extend beyond the historical reporting system so that management intervention is not simply a reaction to income and expenditure trends but pervades every aspect of the management of the resources available.

Significant interventions

Most budget managers contemplate the intervention process with a sense of depression because they associate it with a reduction in financial resources. However, as has been demonstrated, this is not always the case. In order to achieve budgetary objectives and a change in direction, it has been suggested earlier that the use of commitment management techniques is appropriate to both an increase and a decrease in a budget. The mirror imaging of these two extremes is illustrated in Figure 8.5.

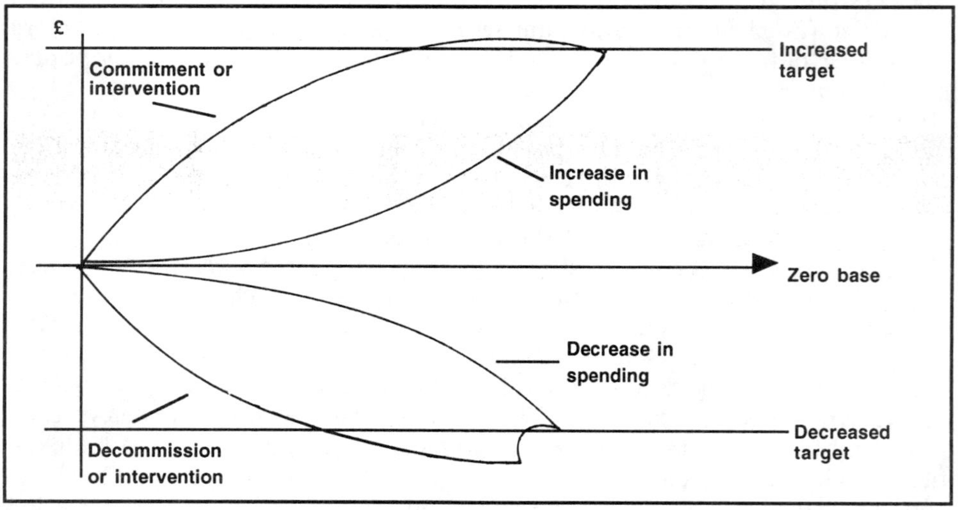

Figure 8.5. Mirror images

The decommission of existing resources is the intervention process that reduces expenditure. It produces characteristics which are similar to the commitment process already discussed but requires the budget manager to conform with predetermined management arrangements which create the necessary resource mobility without undue turbulence or, in the worst case, chaos.

Key points summary

- **Tactical intervention is the main budgetary moderating tool.**
- **Its competent use facilitates the strategic process and is the enabling factor in operational budgetary management.**
- **Intervention is used in:**
  - **Profile compliance.**
  - **Development.**
  - **Retraction.**
- **Its effect is measured in terms of:**
  - **Spending curbs which produce savings.**
  - **Expenditure increases in response to development needs.**
- **Effective intervention is dependent on reliable financial information that is communicated with minimum delay.**
- **Quality financial decisions are dependent on and constrained by conflicting requirements:**
  - **The need for caution when contemplating expenditure.**
  - **The need for expediency as time runs out.**
- **Development and retraction are dependent on resource mobility**

Case study

In the new financial year, because of underspending in the previous year, 'X''s budget was reduced from £2.5m to £2.4m. 'X' had already offered contracts in respect of 11 additional posts to bring the complement up to inspection requirements.

The Treasurer had suggested that staffing could be reduced by natural wastage, but the age profile favoured younger age groups and no retirements were imminent. In addition, staff turnover rates had reduced from around ten per cent in previous years to under five per cent last year. If this downward trend in staff turnover continued, 'X' was doubtful whether the necessary target figure by the end of the year could be met.

The total number of staff, including the new appointments, was 240. If the turnover continued at five per cent then 'X' would lose only 12 staff during the whole year. In an effort to obtain a degree of mobility right at the start of the year, 'X' immediately froze all further vacancies and began to reduce supplementary expenses such as overtime, etc.

To compound the problem, there was a difficulty producing the budget figure for the new year. The figures for May were the first reports issued. These became available in July. The May results indicated that five whole-time equivalent staff were accounting for the over spending (see Table 8.3).

Cumulative budget	Spending	Over spending
£	£	£
401,697	410,276	8,579
(234wte)	(239wte)	(5wte)

Table 8.3. Cumulative budget to May 1994

Applying the formula from August, the first effective intervention date, the savings required would be five whole-time equivalent staff for a full 12 months:

$$Rmt = S \qquad \therefore Rm = S/t.$$

The resource mobility required is therefore [5 ÷ 7 x 12 = 8.57wte].

'X' continued to struggle with this difficult task and managed to curb spending so that at the end of the financial year she had an overspend of £20k. The results for the full year are shown in Table 8.4.

Cumulatives (£m)	Apr	May	Jne	Jly	Aug	Sept	Oct	Nov	Dec	Jan	Feb	Mar
Spending	0.21	0.41	0.62	0.82	1.03	1.24	1.45	1.66	1.85	2.04	2.23	2.42
Budget	0.2	0.4	0.6	0.8	1.0	1.2	1.4	1.6	1.8	2.0	2.2	2.4

Table 8.4. Budget and spending results

Variations are shown in Figure 8.6.

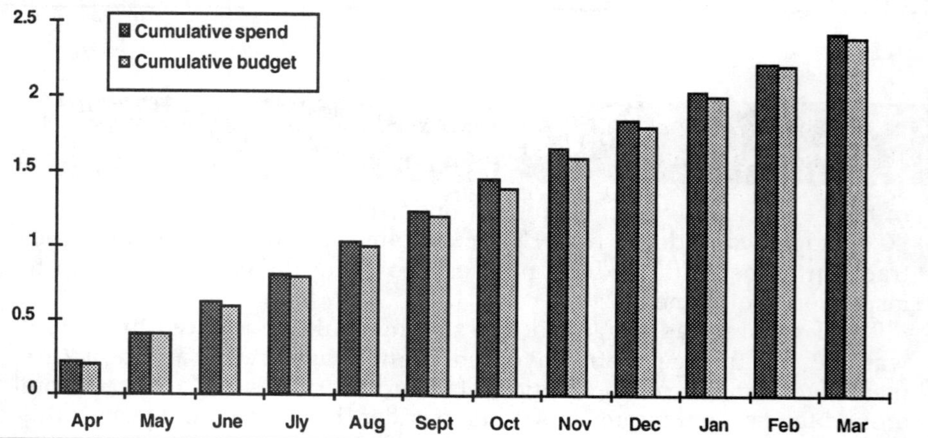

Figure 8.6. Budget and spending variations

Surviving in General Management. Berman and Fielding. Macmillan 1990.

9

Control

Objectives

The purpose of this chapter is to show how the control function operates in the context of budgetary management. The main stages in the business and management model are:

- Business planning for the internal and external environments.
- Contracting and income management for budgetary distribution.
- Profiling and setting budgets.
- Monitoring and measuring progress.
- Intervention at strategic and operational levels.

These stages must be effectively managed and controlled at suitable control points in the processes already outlined. Effective control is the theme developed around a number of examples which:

- demonstrate the capacity of a budget manager to exert control over a wide variety of activities;
- the emphasis is on taking effective action to control these activities;
- consider the extreme case; and
- demonstrate the need for flexibility in control and point to where capacity for control is extinguished.

The chapter is concerned with a balanced and disciplined approach to the control function and is intended to be read as a summary and check on the matters dealt with in previous chapters.

The nature of budgetary control

At one time, the term 'budgetary control' was common currency. Indeed, even today many people still find it difficult to distinguish between managing as opposed to controlling a budget. The notion of budgetary control was appropriate in an era when there was little change. Demands were increasing and public monies were apparently more plentiful. The main objective was to contain that demand. Consequently, the concept of quite simply controlling spending was expounded and devices evolved to facilitate this aim.

The functions necessary to achieve budgetary management have been shown to extend far beyond a simple control technique. They are a response to the changing management style expected from the modern public servant. This does not imply that there is no longer a necessity to control funds. In fact this requirement is more potent now than ever before. There is, however, a change in emphasis both in the interpretation and application of control.

As far as interpretation is concerned, managers must create mobility in order to make changes. This means that they must assure the quality of their decisions and actions so that controlled movement takes place. Conceptually this differs from a definition which implies reign, rule or restraint. For management purposes therefore, a broader meaning which facilitates flexibility must be used.

Managers must be flexible in their approach to quality decisions; they must gain maximum mobility in the resources at their disposal so that they can react to changing financial circumstances and remain in business.

It follows from this broader interpretation that the control function must be evident throughout the management budget process. There must be a perceived equality of distribution within an authority. This aspect is illustrated in Figure 9.1.

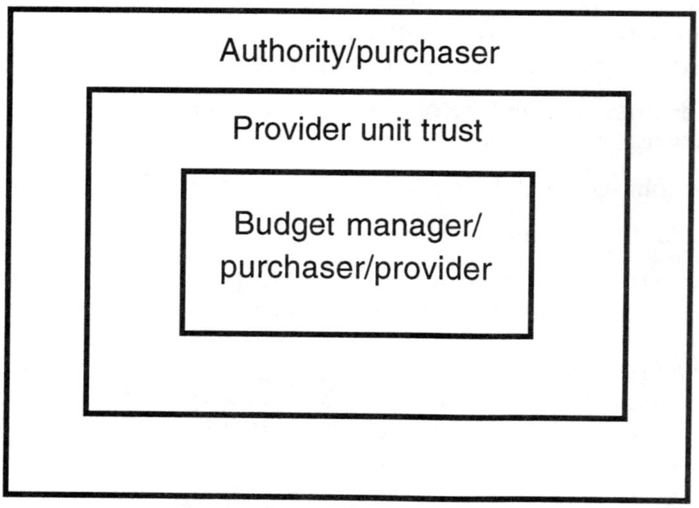

Figure 9.1. Equity distribution

The budget manager is the central pivot upon which achievement is based, but if control is perceived to favour any different level, or to be exercised in a singular way, then the credibility of that control will be damaged. Thus, in total terms, if an authority or budget holder, because budget targets had been achieved, did not seek to exercise control over a manager who did not achieve a target then this would taken by others as a prescription for the future. For example, in Table 9.1 budget managers A, C & D have produced underspendings which taken together exceed B's overspending by 100.

Budget manager	Budget £k	+/- £k
A	60,200	-786
B	145,081	+12,681
C	961,309	-11,772
D	96,500	-223
Totals	1,263,190	-100

Table 9.1. Under and overspending

Effectively B has expended some of the other budget managers' resource shares. If either B, or the general manager, or the authority takes no action to control this trend, it will impair future projects. It can reallocate resources in favour of B on the grounds that other managers are over resourced, unless this action is the result of a plan, it will have the definite disadvantage of disheartening the other managers.

B has a number of options which facilitate control:

- seek a reallocation of resources on the grounds of inequality;
- make a bid on reserve monies on the grounds of increased workload;
- seek bridging finance;
- demonstrate clear difficulties in achieving objectives over a greater time span;
- create an increase in workload which would attract additional resources; and
- show how the deficit may be made good by increasing income.

The general manager has a number of options:

- it might be decided to accept B's explanation for the overspending on the grounds that B has either been previously disadvantaged;
- this would mean that B's position would be tolerated in the expectation of improvement;
- additional resources would have to be allocated from reserves;
- it might be neccessary to access bridging finance in order to facilitate B in accomplishing objectives;
- steps might be taken which would reduce B's budget responsibilities, or would completely relieve B of responsibility.

Controlling the supply chain

Purchasing decisions may be taken deliberately or passively, and their impact may therefore happen according to plan or by default. Acquiescence is not in all cases to be condemned, however, for much in the purchasing world is repetitive.

Each expenditure feature, as shown in Figure 9.1, must therefore be clearly identified and anticipated as a final episode. In arranging activities into an expected sequence it is possible to distinguish between items which arise from conscious decision taking and those which are the result of acquiescence. As well as this, where no conscious management decision has been taken, there is clearly no real delay in acquiring such items. Thus, while there is a saving in time, financial resources can be under threat.

The main threat of public purchasing policy, whether it relates to human or other resources, is to reduce as far as possible unstructured spending and to move towards purchases which can be regulated by formal contracts. However, this movement creates a problem for the budget holder because the length of the supply chain tends to cause delay in fulfilling procurement of a particular resource.

On the one hand the time spectrum can be shortened through repeat orders, unreviewed work patterns, metered changes or stock issues, and on the other, a complex contracting procedure can considerably elongate the time taken to fulfil a decision. There are therefore two terminal facets—increased activity and potential decline in standards which should be controlled. However, if these are not coordinated, unacceptable financial consequences may result.

In order to take advantage of their considerable purchasing power, public authorities, either individually or collectively, provide for their resource procurement arrangements through dedicated departments or directorates. These departments are generally divided into:

- personnel for staffing;
- estate services for all matters relating to property and engineering; and
- general purchasing for other goods and services.

Depending on the type of public services, there may be other departments which are necessary in order to comply with legislation. For example, in health care, drugs would be purchased by the pharmacy and dispensed on prescription by the doctor.

An example of a typical spread of purchasing over various directorate is shown in Table 9.2. Taking as an example a small acute hospital where in addition to the purchasing directorates mentioned, the pharmacy would already be included, the business split is as shown in the table.

Purchasing directorates

Budget headings	Personnel £k	Supplies £k	Pharmacy £k	Estates £k	HQ £k	Totals £k
Direct patient care						
Clinical directorates	8,528	580	682		92	9,882
Theatre manager	557	120	103			780
Outpatients manager	345	35	80			460
Radiology	480	310	50			840
Physiotherapy	256	17				273
Pathology	722	201	80			1,003
Sub totals	**10,888**	**1,263**	**995**	**0**	**92**	**13,238**
Hotel services						
Catering	599	397				996
Laundry & linen	108	115				223
Domestic	530	251				781
Portering	240	50				290
General services	88	237				325
Sub totals	**1,565**	**1,050**	**0**	**0**	**0**	**2,615**
Estate services						
Maintenance	281			879		1,160
Heat/light	51				394	445
Other charges					724	724
Sub totals	**332**	**0**	**0**	**879**	**1,118**	**2,329**
Information services	880	140			201	1,221
Totals	**13,665**	**2,453**	**995**	**879**	**1,411**	**19,403**

Table 9.2. Business split between purchasing directorates and pharmacy

From this, it can be seen that purchasing directorates' share of business is as shown in Table 9.3.

	£k	£k
Personnel	13,665	
Supplies	2,453	
Pharmacy	995	
Estates	879	
HQ	1,411	19,403

Table 9.3. Purchasing directorates' share of business

This business is attracted from budget holders under the four main headings shown in Table 9.4.

	£k	£k
Direct patient care	13,238	
Hotel services	2,615	
Estate services	2,329	
Information services	1,221	19,403

Table 9.4

Each directorate will be professionally managed and, depending on its volume of business, will enter into contracts for particular resource requirements. These contracts will be pitched at international, national, regional or local level, as appropriate. For example, special equipment might be purchased from an international contract, petrol and oil from a national, furniture from a regional, and vegetables from a local contract. Contracts for human resources, on the other hand, will usually access terms and conditions negotiated nationally, but offer and acceptance will depend on local recruitment and selection procedures.

The objective is to obtain the best value for money through competition, and contractual formality will depend on the value of services to be provided.

Although it can be seen that, in each case, the purchasing process is managed by an independent department, the budget manager must participate at various stages so that contracted services are delivered at the

- right place;
- right time; and
- right price.

This means that a considerable investment in terms of time and patience is necessary on the part of the budget holders so that they derive longer-term benefits. The length of the supply chain is therefore relevant to the achievement of overall budgetary control so that sight is not lost of earlier commitments which may take time to progress from the initial stages through to fulfilment and payment.

Budget managers must enter into a tripartite control arrangement which will secure coordination between the treasury and purchasing departments. This tripartite arrangement is illustrated in Figure 9.2.

In order to shorten the delays in fulfilling a resource requirement it is possible to clear as much of the preparatory work as possible before the episode takes place. In addition, during the episode, budget holders expeditiously clear paper work so that the various stages are properly regulated and payment is made at the proper time or, in the event of a difficulty arising as to the quality, quantity or price, that this is attended to without delay. Failure to do so may cost money.

Some of the major events in which a budget holder must be involved are illustrated in Figure 9.3.

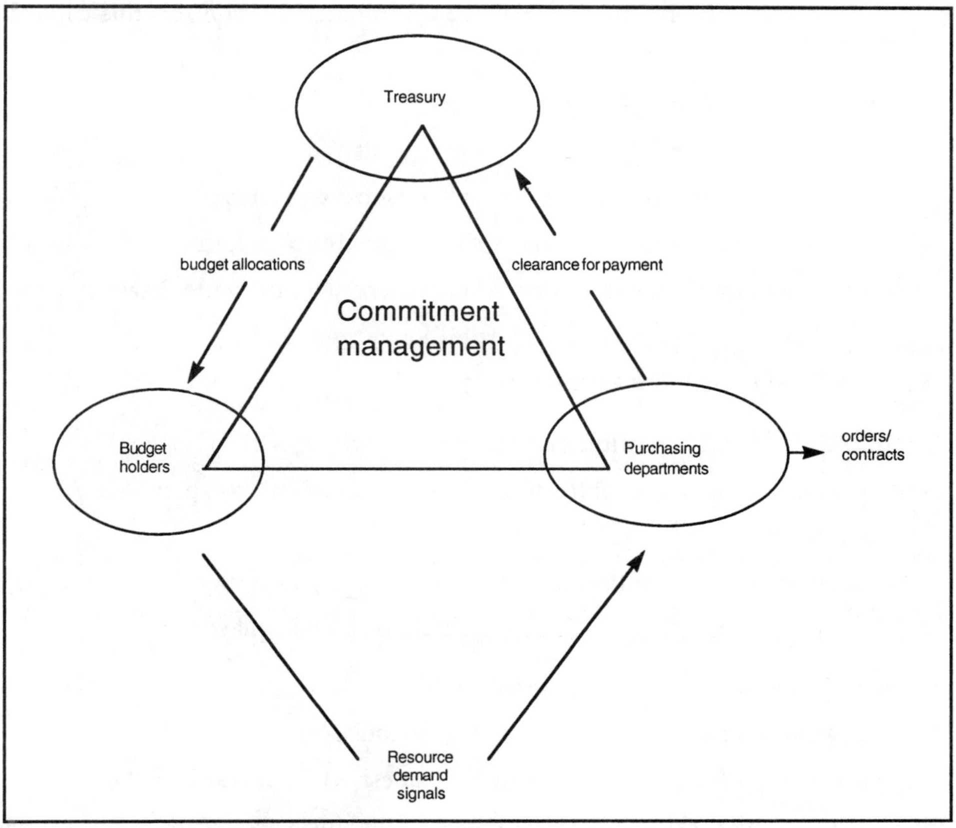

Figure 9.2. Supply chain participation

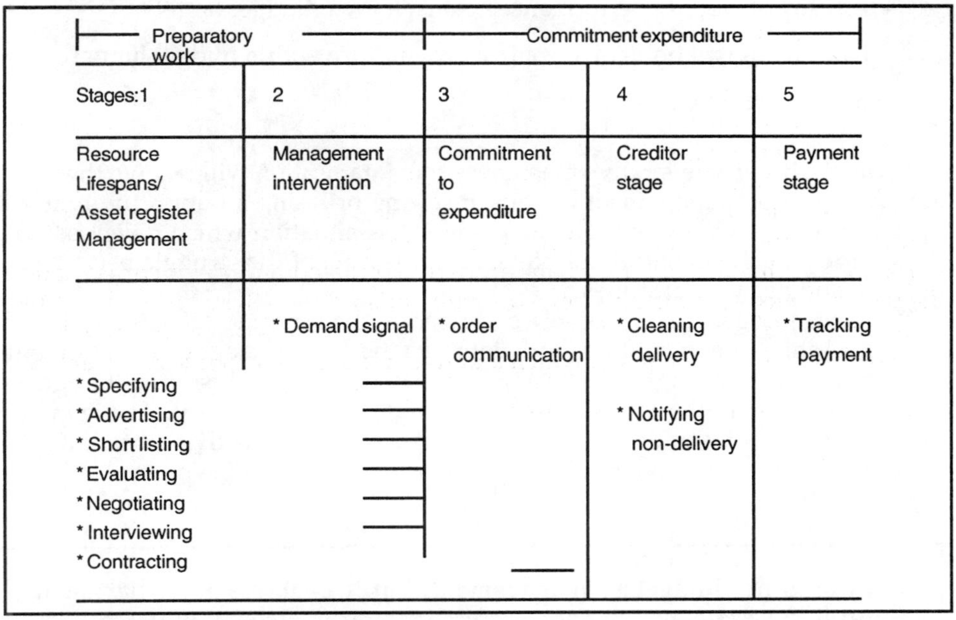

Figure 9.3. Stage control points

The developing information base which coordinates and controls this tripartite interface will:

1. **Facilitate budget holders in:**
   - controlling expenditure within known limits;
   - deciding which expenditure options must have priority;
   - monitoring committed orders against expenditure patterns;
   - selecting other buying options where delivery times cannot be met;
   - achieving better buying and distribution targets; and
   - rendering improved accountability;
2. **Improve overall commitment management which will:**
   - provide an overview of the total UOM commitment to expenditure;
   - control goods and services expenditure;
   - facilitate instant monitoring;
   - indicate areas where resource distribution can take place.
3. **Assist the purchasing department in:**
   - determining the scope of business in financial terms;
   - accessing information on potential business which is transacted elsewhere;
   - managing workloads against expected business as expressed in budget volumes;
   - measuring buying performance against known budget targets;
   - helping budget holders to control expenditure within budget limits;
   - improving total accountability.

Through this administrative machinery the organisation will resolve these two apparently incompatible instincts, but in seizing or losing an opportunity it will tend to progress or decline. The evolving stress situation which develops with the progress of the financial episode is characteristic of the struggle between the positive and negative attitudes.

The control aspect can be loosely described as the time and effort spent in processing an item of expenditure, and embraces the various stages from the identification of need, through purchasing and payment to the historical budgetary impact, and later to the care and treatment of the patient or client. As the quality of the latter aspect is an irrevocable consequence of earlier activity it follows that the control of earlier activities must be seen as part of the whole process.

Control is not budgetary management, but it is an essential part of it. Control causes delay. It must therefore include an element of flexibility

Control context

The control context must be seen in the relationship between the various roles of:

- the purchaser;
- the resource manager;
- the service provider; and
- the interfaces beween them.

These facets are illustrated in Figure 9.4 .

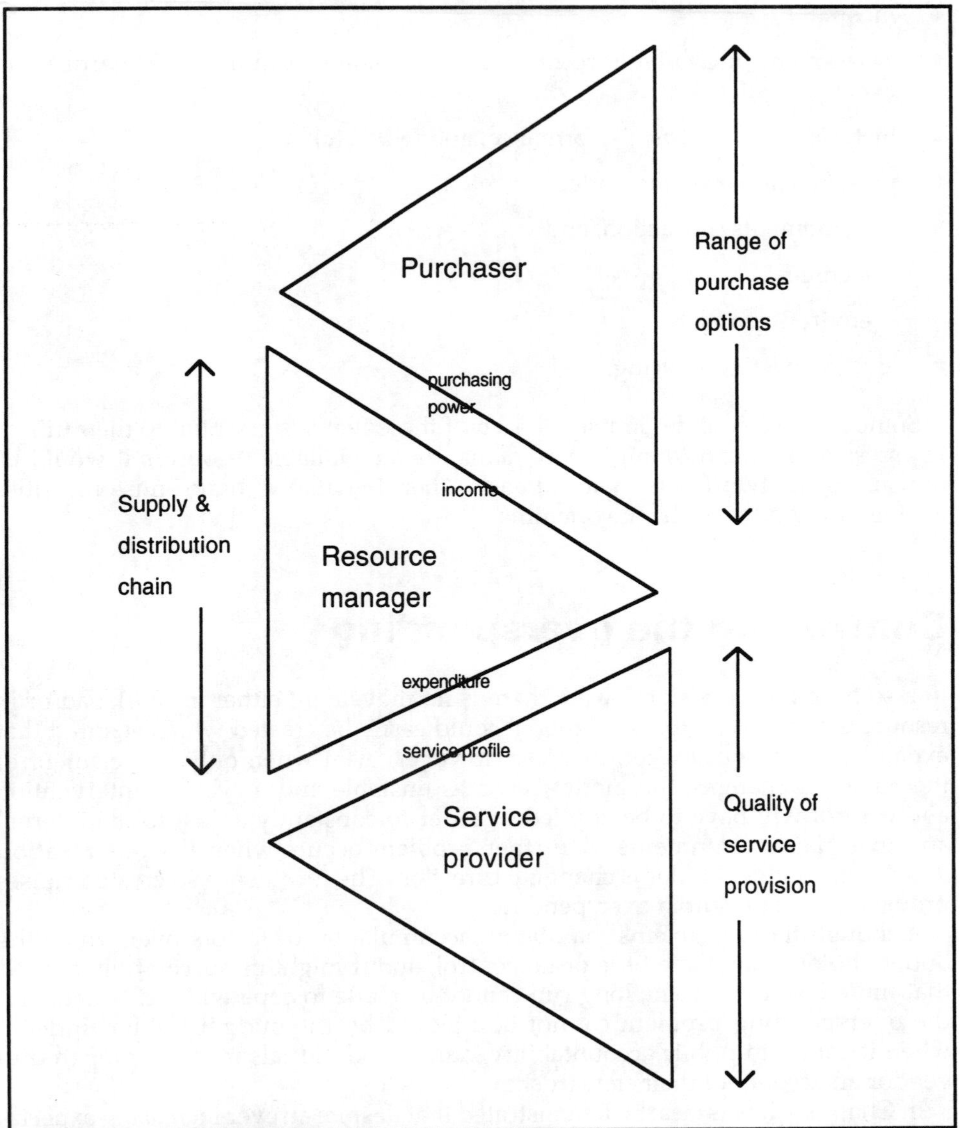

Figure 9.4. Control interfaces

Some or all of the roles may be combined into one function and the manager's conflict in the management of the control function needs to be clarified:

- the rationalisation of roles in exercising options to purchase—as a purchaser;
- the management of the supply chain—as a resource manager; and
- the effective provision of an acceptable service profile—as a service provider.

This consultative and continuous planning and control process must incorporate some indication of:

- external environmental considerations;
- market share;
- income;
- assessment of available resources: time, estate, equipment, expertise and expendibles;
- historical legacy (past performance, goodwill, etc);
- present standards (their adequacy etc);
- developments/retraction; and
  - technical
  - environmental
- level of existing funding.

Some indication of the impact of each of these items is essential to their utility. In assessing and controlling future demands on available resources it would be unusual if the two facets matched each other. Inevitably compromise priorities evolve through the exchange dilemma.

Controlling the overspending

In a so called 'steady state', were there is no movement either in workload or in resources available, a financial model could easily be created which ensured that expenditure did not exceed income. However, even when only one element of the equation changes, the model becomes unstable and a cycle of intervention and control will have to be applied in order to constantly adjust to the internal and external environments. A further problem occurs when the organisation and/or the budget holder is changing direction. The turbulence so created causes problems which result in overspendings.

Although these problems may be an accumulation of factors over which the budget holder may have little or no control, and it might be successfully argued that finite resources in the long run cannot be made to cope with finite demand, the overspending problem cannot be ignored by the budget holder. Indeed, when it comes to public accountability, named individuals must be prepared to vendor an account of their stewardship.

In Chapter 4 it was clearly demonstrated that despite an ever increasing expectation of improved performance to a point where budget managers may be expected to wind up all or part of their businesses, the need to live within resources available must have priority. While issues pertaining to the quality of services will be ventilated, inevitably the budget manager cannot afford to ignore the financial consequences of procrastination. This section is intended to provide some guidelines which will be helpful in forming an action plan for management intervention.

There are three fundamental causes for an overspending:

- income shortfalls;
- increased spending; or
- a combination of both.

Conterminous with these causes are three basic questions which a budget manager needs to answer

- Is it real?
- Is it significant?
- What are my options?

Discovery of the cause often reveals the answers to the first two questions. In other words, it is important to counterbalance the possibility of over-reaction to an overspending by rationalisation of its causes with reality and significance. It must be emphasised, however, that many managers' failure can be attributed to their preoccupation with this facet. They may become engrossed, for example, with underfunding issues and are either indifferent to or neglectful of the dominant necessity to bring the budget into balance.

Contemplation of an overspending must therefore be subjected to a four-stage process, which:

- assesses the need for intervention in a structured way;
- determines what action is necessary;
- activates intervention; and
- reviews and corrects.

Assessment

The following steps should be taken by the budget manager:

- Identify the problem area.
- Check calculations to ensure that no mistake has been made.
- Decide whether the overspending is due to:
  - continuous but predictable budget (see Figure 6.1, p 75);
  - development/retraction modes (see Figure 6.2, p 76);
  - the impact of casual expenditure (see Figure 6.3, p 77);
  - infrequent but predictable expenditure (see Figure 6.4, p 78); or
  - an irregularity in budget profiling (see Figure 6.5, p 79).
- Examine budget targets to ensure that all income has been properly credited.

- Examine the outstanding commitments position.
- Check all budget remainders and decide whether some reallocations can be made.
- Decide whether further intervention is necessary.
- Always keep finance colleagues informed and make sure that there is proper documentation.

Calculations checklist

- Check contract details against budget target figure to ensure that all agreed credits have been included.
- Check all totals and variances calculations.
- Check dates and time-scales.
- Check previous performance against current overspending to measure the scale of current overspending.
- Check scale of current overspending against current allocation to ensure that all monies due are credited and that no additional funding can be attracted.
- Check all supplementary data:
  - overtime;
  - sickness;
  - extra duty, etc,

  and ensure that these amounts reflect what has been approved.
- Check work-loads to see whether there has been an increase in demand, or a development which should attract additional funds.
- Check staff numbers against names to ensure that no irregularities have been changed.
- Check (were available) all supporting data.

Check the equations; although it is not possible to be specific about the variety of financial and related equations that pervade the public service, in general terms there are two basic principles which can be tested. These relate to the financial balance and to the rate of consumption or production. The **financial balance** is obtained by subtracting expenditure from income and this is a consistent theme throughout any budgetary management mechanism. The **rate of consumption/production** is obtained by dividing the value allocated or spent by the number of units. This gives a cost or average cost.

The **check** is made by comparing one result with the other, thus if we are told that £100,000 (£100k) will buy ten staff per annum it is reasonable to expect that this can be tested as a period progresses. To simplify this at the end of the period.

This does not really require a calculation to demonstrate that one or a number of things are wrong. The bottom line is that the budget is marginally overspent, yet all the resources theoretically allocated have not been consumed.

The financial balance is shown to be:

Amount allocated	Actually spent	Balance of overspending
£100,000	£101,000	£1000 (+)

The rate of consumption is shown to be:

Funded staff level	Staff actually employed	Variation
10	9.7	-0.3

Figure 9.5.

The Check

- The allocated or assumed average cost per staff number is £10,000 (£10k).
- The average amount consumed is £101,000/9.7 (£10,412 (£10(+)k)).
- The difference is (-) 0.3 staff should have released a saving of £3,000 (£3k).

This anomaly should have been apparent as the year progressed and there are a number of possible causes. For example:

- the budget was under funded by £4,120;
- the manager failed to buy staff at the correct level; and
- compensation for staff losses during the year occurred in overtime and other payments in order to keep the service maintained; etc.

Key points summary

- Control is an essential part of the total budget management process.
- Excessive control can cause delay: this can be used to advantage but it can also stifle the process.
- Managers must establish clearly where effective control can be exercised so that caution and expedition can be properly balanced.
- The main interfaces are concerned with resource limitations within the contracts.
- Budget contract conditions in most organisations seldom can be found in one document.
- Performance measures and control points are usually found in a collection of reports.
- Budget managers must not assume that information will automatically be made available.
- They must ensure that delays and difficulties cause minimum disruption.
- Budget managers must ensure that minimum contract data sets come regularly into their possession.
- Activities must be controlled within the context, intervention and outcomes assessed and reviewed.
- The budget holder must have:
  - terms and conditions of the contract;
  - scope and range of the services to be provided;
  - budget price and financial constraints;
  - relevant purchasing power catalogues;
  - cost of output; and
  - management audit facilities.

They must develop the discipline of cross checking calculations at each control stage and comparing real with expected profiles.

Part 3

Synopsis—Developing and measuring competence

It has been seen that the individual budget manager's behaviour is both constrained and influenced by the internal and external environments. In order to maximise the benefits to be derived from management action managers must react to their environments in a systematic way. Taking these factors together, the manager must achieve a certain performance level, as shown in the diagram below.

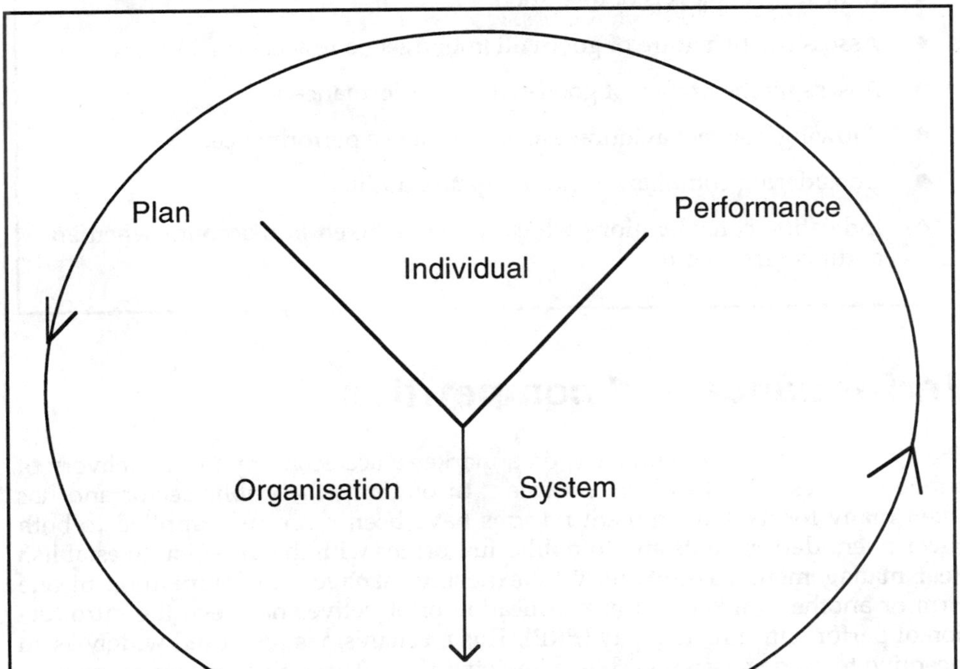

We cannot measure this performance unless all the factors are taken into account. In short, we need to define what we mean by performance and then see whether measurement is possible.

10

Performance management

Objectives

The purpose of this chapter is to explore the concepts of performance in the context of competition. This is examined by:

- Identifying the expectation for improvement.
- Indicating the levels of toleration.
- Assessing the nature of goodwill in budget contracts.
- Assessing the impact of good-will on performance.
- Showing how behavioural aspects influence performance.
- Considering compliance and budgetary audit.
- Indicating considerations which must be taken into account when an audit is carried out.

Performance and competition

The 1980s saw a greater emphasis on a market-place economy in the delivery of public services. This has been prevalent throughout the public sector and has taken many forms. Government reforms have been rigorously applied to both government departments and to public authorities with the intention to establish clear management accountability by exposing managers to competition in one form or another. Linked to this clarification of objectives has been the introduction of performance-related pay (PRP). This mechanism is now used widely as an incentive to managers who achieve key objectives. Through a system of individual performance review (IPR) their achievements are banded to reflect the degree of their success or otherwise. Where managers are perceived to fail in achieving their objectives, their future will be jeopardised because their employment condition is dependent on short-term contracts which may not be renewed.

In parallel with this has been the general development of a competitive element in the public sector. Market forces have been brought to bear upon numerous services. Examples can be found in competitive tendering for catering, cleaning and highway construction, where managers of services had to compete with private companies. The result was that a number of private concerns were successful thus opening up a new market place. Plans are now in hand to extend this[1].

The introduction of the market-place has also been accomplished by the separation of policy divisions from service providers. This approach has been applied to the NHS, personal social services and some parts of the Civil Service. The separation of purchaser and seller functions is intended to:

- define service provision;
- identify costs;
- alleviate the purchaser's dependence on a single provider
- facilitate competition between providers; and
- encourage new entrants into the market.

Other initiatives which are intended to improve performance are privatisation, decentralisation and the recognition of the customer through the Citizen's Charter.

Inherent in all these initiatives is the government's determination to achieve better value for money. Public expenditure plans are published together with measures of expected performance such as costs and volumes of activity. Through this mechanism comparisons and deductions about relative efficiency can be made. More vigorous and systematic examination of performance has been facilitated through the establishment of the Audit Commission which reviews local authority and NHS performance. The Audit Commission reports greatly facilitate work of various House of Commons select committees which frequently put penetrating questions to senior public servants about performance. The exposure of costs and general performance to public scrutiny is therefore a significant modifying influence on spending.

At national level it might be concluded that the parameters for performance in the public sector would follow a general pattern which broadly indicate:

- the incidence of public expenditure (for example, money spent per region, area, unit);
- levels and range of resources committed, for example the number of teachers, nurses, police, buses, etc;
- the prevalence of deprivation; and
- evidence of competition and cost comparisons.

Budget managers operating at local level are clearly exposed to these initiatives and comparisons. They make significant contributions to overall performance.

Budget managers' performance in turn is closely linked to general objectives and measures.

Expectation

In a paper entitled 'Limiting Factors in Budget Contracts' attention was drawn to the quality of budgetary management in the context of performance[2]. The harmony that exists between expectation and results was perceived to be an attempted improvement in condition, earlier referred to as the creation of a surplus in the availability of some or all of the resources at a budget manager's disposal.

This, it has been demonstrated, will occur mainly through a movement or a change in direction in the way things are managed, with mutual benefit derived both by the budget manager and the organisation. However, the debilitating effects of the ageing process upon acquired assets, together with potentially inept management, can prejudice both expectation and the actual result. In these conditions it often happens that an increasing difference occurs between the expectation and the result.

The incidence of this phenomenon, although generally experienced in degraded mode, is fairly common. In a natural dynamic state, budget managers will complain about resource shortages and underfunding issues and the business organisation in pursuit of efficiency and effectiveness will be even more demanding. Both these objectives should be viewed as one and the same thing which through the corporate budget plan are resolved into a common mission. There is, in effect, a toleration of both points of view.

This toleration of expectation can, however, move as time progresses from modest demands placed on the budget manager to a point where a sense of unreality may prevail. Increasing expectation can be expressed in terms of actual or perceived past performance.

In budgetary terms increased expectation can result in a progressive reduction of budgetary capacity which ultimately, if nothing else happens, will result in a gradual increase in an overspending. If this were to be the only performance measure used, then significant damage would be caused to the budgetary management system in that expectation would have at some point become unrealistic and the capacity of the manager to achieve surpluses, invalidated. Manifestly unfair treatment of a potentially high performer quickly leads to dissatisfaction and may pose a significant threat to systematic credibility.

Goodwill

Although sight must not be lost of the spending position of both the budget manager and the organisation as a whole, it is apparent that a number of other factors impact on the capacity to live within a particular budget dimension. These may be brought together into a collection of factors which are often referred to as goodwill. The paper 'Goodwill as a consideration in Budget Contracts' sets out the parameters which may assist managers in evaluating the goodwill content[3]. In common with many other budget characteristics, evidence of the 'goodwill factor' may not be apparent in a situation where there is minimal change. However, increases in expectation which go beyond the normal tensions created in a real situation to a point were the organisation applies undue pressure to its a contractual obligations, or were the budget manager fails to adequately participate, can precipitate this evidence.

At such a point it might be that no redress is possible, and the budget contract would be invalidated. It follows, therefore, that managers are made well aware of the implications and the value of goodwill so that no such critical situation can be allowed to occur. The reciprocal arrangements which exists between 'management' and the budget manager are often observed to mature over the years. From a management point of view concessions to the budget manager may be balanced with the budget manager's perspective, where account must be taken of achievements.

There are various definitions which can be applied to goodwill. In legal terms it is sometimes taken to be 'nothing more than the probability that old customers will resort to the old place' and sometimes 'the benefit arising from connection and reputation'.

In accounting terms this can be translated into the capacity to make a surplus after certain changes have been made. As goodwill never appears in books of account except where a business has been purchased, a new partner has been introduced, or an old partner has departed, it is apparent that from a public service point of view, its calculation, although relevant to this discussion, has few precedents. It is also clear that calculations are usually completed only when a change in direction occurs.

Applying the partnership criteria, however, it is possible to achieve a goodwill base-line rating through allocating points for budget bulk. In this context the paper 'Limiting Factors in Budget Contracts' drew attention to the relationship which exists between the number of budget managers and the total value of resources available. This relationship can be expressed in the equation:

Total available resources = {No. of budget managers} x {selective value of delegated resource quotas}.

As the available resources are finite and therefore constant, it follows that if the number of budget managers increases then the selective value of delegated resource quotas (the size of each budget) will fall. In a situation where there are too many budget managers, budget sizes and capacity for movement will be diminished. There will therefore, in consequence, be a significant impact upon the goodwill rating. For this reason, budget focus, discussed earlier, is all the more important.

It is difficult to be prescriptive about desirable budget sizes. In a climate where there is little change, budget sizes do not have the same impact. Except that small recurring expenditure budgets (say less than £50k per annum) are notoriously difficult to manage mainly because of the significant problems inherent in replacement/recruitment and absenteeism. Where a climate of change prevails, and this is currently prevalent in the public service, experience indicates that budget sizes which promote both resource mobility and goodwill should be in excess of £1m although clearly the dictates of a particular activity will be a dominant situation.

Participation

Budget managers may themselves inhibit the effectiveness of a system through the manifestation of open hostility, or through latent and subversive opposition to the direction being taken. In the paper 'Non Participating Budget Holders' it is argued that a system which did not exhibit any ability for self scrutiny in this context fostered complacency, and therefore lacked capacity to fully realise budget management potential[4]. It is important, therefore, that in such an instance, where goodwill is perceived to have diminished, evidence is available so that damage is limited.

This is clearly a sensitive area because, on the one hand, a dynamic organisation needs to look objectively at various options—even if they are distasteful—but on the other, consistently destructive opposition becomes increasingly difficult to manage. In addition to this, an organisation's increasing expectations and consequently its demands on budget holders may themselves be contributing factors to this disillusionment. It is important therefore to make a distinction between organisational politics and the impact that open or latent hostility may have on goodwill.

In addition to this feature, it can happen in the public service that budget managers have discovered that, in the past, it has been possible to overspend a budget and find satisfactory reasons for that overspending. To compound this, misinformation may also be present regarding the infinite size of the public purse and the notion that underspendings are forever losses to the budget manager. The central theme in these situations concerns the way in which budget managers imagine they can protect and enhance their budgetary share.

An overview of a system may therefore infer that some budget managers are non-participators, whereas, in fact, they may be manipulating the system by working through a sub-agenda. In budgetary terms, these features are collectively regarded as hostile. Hostility can be open or latent. The paper 'Non Participating Budget Holders' identifies five factors which contributed to this situation[5]. They are:

- genuine fear or abhorrence of financial matters;
- inability to manage;
- professional dignity;
- laziness; and
- confidence.

Where these factors are represented in terms of open (o) or latent (L) hostility, ranges of hostility prevalence might be found to be weighted:

- Fear o>L.
- Inability L>o.
- Dignity o>L.
- Laziness L>o.
- Confidence L>o.

The connection between expectation and hostility might be observed to be:-

Expectation tends to NIL when latent hostility is prevalent

It is clear that management must be prepared to react to this type of situation and the valuation of goodwill, both in terms of philosophy and practice, will dominate the argument.

The link between expectation and past performance in the valuation of goodwill has therefore been demonstrated and can be expressed in the equation $Ep=f^*(P(t-1))$, where Ep is expected performance and $P(t-1)$ is taken to be previous performance. If the function f^* was taken to be very near or equal to unity then clearly expectation and past performance will be equal. In effect, this would be a perfect model in which goodwill would be discounted through minimal change, and expectation would be the same as actual performance.

However, where changes in budget structure are a feature, the goodwill in referring surpluses for other developments is an important consideration in maximising a budget manager's performance. In the case were a budget manager was expected to live within a decreasing budget, the expectation component in financial terms would be expressed.

In this situation there are five component parts:

- Original budget base (o).
- Expected degree of compression (E).
- Revised budget target (T).
- Actual performance (P).
- Validation between performance and target (v).

A number of simple equations can be derived using these components

$$o - E = T$$
$$A - v = T$$
$$\therefore \; o - E = A - v$$
$$\therefore \; o = A - v + E$$

If the original budget is taken to be 100 per cent, the other figures can be expressed in percentage terms. Table 10.1 below illustrates a few simple examples.

Periods	**2**	**3**	**1**
	%	%	%
Original budget	100	100	100
Expected compression	30	40	20
Revised budget target	70	60	80
Actual performance	90	80	90
Variation	20	20	10

Table 10.1. Budgets expressed in percentage terms

In diagrammatic form this is shown in Figure 10.1.

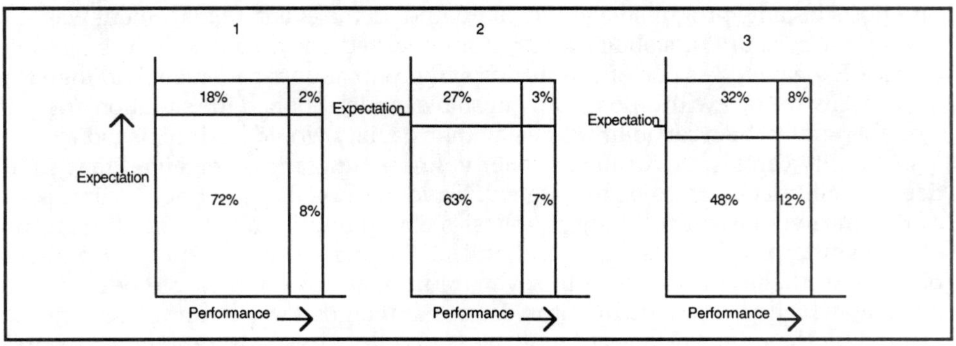

Figure 10.1. Budgets expressed in percentage terms

In all these cases the performance levels fall below the revised budget target and there are overspendings.

The dilemma exists, however, as to which figure actually represents goodwill. On the one hand, each budget rendered a surplus based on the original budget and, on the other, none of them conformed with the expected compression. Strictly speaking, the goodwill valuation would be based on the surplus actually created but in performance terms the achievements would not be acceptable.

Assuming that this was the same budget, examined over a three-year period, it will be observed that the expected compression is progressive, moving between 20 per cent in the first year, through 30 per cent in the second to 40 per cent in the third year. The budget is in fact in a retracting mode. Surpluses stayed static in the first two years at ten per cent and increased to 20 per cent in the third year. The goodwill in executing and delivering the desired outcome was therefore diminishing although performance was improving. In organisational terms, whatever the peripheral issues, the budget manager is not conforming to the budget plan. The 'common ground' which lies between expectation and performance is therefore an indication of the goodwill rating and consequently goodwill as an expression of the relationship between management and the budget manager can be valued in terms of:

$$\frac{T \times A}{O}$$

In percentage terms for each year this would be:

Year 1 80 x 90÷100 = 72
Year 2 70 x 90÷100 = 63
Year 3 60 x 80÷100 = 48

These broad indicators take account of both budget size and hostility factors. For example, in *Surviving in General Management*[6] I describe the financial implications of an alteration in the balance of health care which required the development of a retraction model in acute hospital bed provision with commensurate revenue savings of £0.25m. The central pivot of the model proposed the closure of Skegatilla Hospital to be achieved, in stages, over a six-month period. In order to create the necessary resource mobility, all posts which became vacant through natural wastage were frozen and only those which were essential were filled on the basis of temporary contracts. Despite considerable union opposition, it became increasingly difficult to maintain staffing levels in the hospital because existing staff were more and more successful in attaining other posts and prospective candidates for the temporary posts became progressively difficult to find. In the event, management was able to create a measure of stability through internal redeployment. This was possible, because Skegatilla was one of a large hospital group and management had therefore the capacity to cope with a potentially unstable model, but had the situation arisen in a smaller group, then capability to deal with instability would be diminished.

Instability can also occur in customer volumes where it is perceived that a particular facility is likely to be threatened. 'Save our hospital / school...' campaigns can themselves be self-fulfilling prophesies where public anxiety about the future of a hospital or school is expressed and at the same time prospective patients, parents or clients may choose to sever traditional links and create new referral patterns which favour a competitor. These campaigns may therefore be cynically viewed by the upper reaches of management whose desire to rationalise a public service can be enhanced.

There are therefore two main pressures on management to keep the life span of a particular resource within manageable limits. These are:

- a desire to have mobility; and
- the cost of prolonging a life span beyond its realistic use.

Careful consideration of these factors suggests that there is a need to adequately identify and control them. This implies that budgetary control mechanisms must extend beyond the historical reporting system so that management intervention is not simply a reaction to income and expenditure trends but pervades every aspect of the management of the resources which are available.

Audit

- Budgetary audit is generally carried out in a collegiate forum in which the experiences of 'management', budget managers and finance staff are shared.
- The purpose of this forum is to discover best practice and to seek compliance from all participants on a programme of work which will achieve value for money in the public service.
- It is important that the forum has both structure and independent support so that a meaningful evaluation can be carried out.
- The audit will embrace the activities of organisation, system and budget managers, but specific issues and problems experienced by individual managers will be confidential unless that manager decides otherwise.

The audit agenda will move through the traditional cycle shown in Figure 10.2.

- Discovery of existing standards and protocols.
- Testing for compliance with standards protocols.
- Discovery of irregularities in compliance.
- Making recommendations for improvements.
- Reviewing progress.

Figure 10.2. The audit cycle

Audit would be set out in a format approximating Table 10.2.

Audit cycle	Organisation	System	Manager
Existing standards & protocols	• Organisational structure • Documentation on corporate plan & evidence of integration in budget targets • Degree of declaration & authority to budget managers • Budget sizes & goodwill assessment	• System cost • Acceptability criteria • System flexibility & degree of sophistication necessary to support corporate plan	• Involvement in & commitment to Corporate Planning Objectives • Evidence of action plan to meet objectives
Compliance	• Testing structure: – plans – contracts • Analysis of organisational ability & determination to meet overall budget objectives	• System benefits & deficiencies • Testing degree of support for plan	• Managers' achievements • Problems in meeting planning objectives • Managers' commentary
Irregularities	• Analysis of organisational strengths & weaknesses in setting & meeting objectives • Budget viability	• Customer deficiencies	• Managers' performance
Recommendations	• Improvements in: – structure – planning – contracting • Changes in: – delegation & – budgetary sizes • Review of spending authority	• Proposals for system refinement & development	• Management development programme dedicated to improve performance
Review	• Analysis of progress to date • Identification of outstanding issues		

Table 10.2. Budgetary audit outline

Key points summary

- The main performance measure that will be applied to individual budget managers is their ability to contain expenditure within their budget.
- This is the most visible sign of their effectiveness.
- However, it has been shown that their activities in cost terms together with the incidence of demand are also important factors.
- Other influences which will affect the outcome of various stages in the process of budgetary management.
- Customer definition and market research.
- Ability to live within available resources and to mobilise those resources to tackle emerging problems.

  Yields capabilities in terms of:

  — quality;

  — quantity;

  — cost and;

  — price.
- A more business-like approach to budget management is inherent in a prevailing culture.
- Practising managers who require knowledge and the development of financial management skills need also an insight into the total picture at local, regional and national level.
- Throughout this process, the budget manager is driven on by competition both externally and from within.

In order to meet the challenge of the market, budget managers compete for their share of custom and for scarce resources.

References

1. CM1730, HM Treasury, November 1991.
2. Limiting factors in budget contracts, W. J. Bryans 1991.
3. Goodwill as a consideration in budget contracts, W. J. Bryans 1992.
4. Non-participating budget holders, W. J. Bryans 1979.
5. *Surviving in General Management*. Berman and Fielding, 1990.

11

Performance and the budget manager

Objectives

The purpose of this chapter is to show in some detail how a budget manager's performance may be measured. It covers how a budget manager can use these measures to improve performance. Specifically, it relates to:

- Work-load measurements and performance.
- Policy and general financial constraints.
- The effects of size, scope and direction of spend on comparative costs.
- Resource mixtures and financial preference.
- Impact of staff morale on the budget manager's performance.
- Measurements and indicators of morale levels.

Introduction

There are a number of ways in which a budget manager's performance can be measured. These mainly relate to the rate at which resources are consumed and the impact that this has upon the budget manager's objectives. For example, if we only examine the degree a particular level of spending varies from the budget, we fail to relate this to the work being done.

We may pay four men for two days and find that the wall has not been built or that the work was shoddy.

Also, it may later be found that another contractor could have undertaken the task and offered a more cost effective quality product.

Although a task may be completed with apparent speed and efficiency, over a period of time it may be found to be defective. Later examination or testing may question the efficiency of a particular technique. This kind of testing is now prevalent in many aspects of the public service where it has been developed into a method of professional audit. Here peer review of outcome often reveals standards of best practice which in turn may be converted into codes of practice. In general terms, therefore, budget managers have at their disposal a range of performance measures, which Figure 11.1 illustrates.

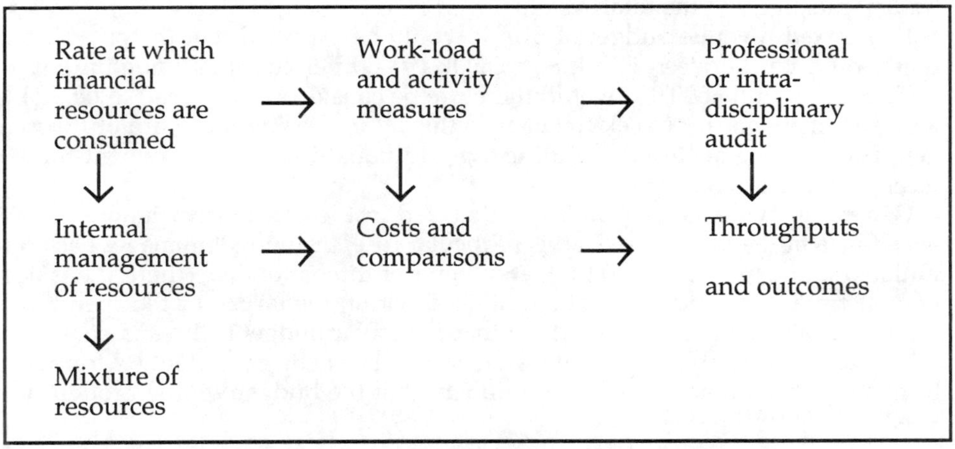

Figure 11.1. Performance measures available to budget managers

The budget manager must act within the spending direction set by the authority. Internal management of resources at their disposal must therefore be subjected by budget managers to the overall regulations established by the authority. This means that whatever action they take must conform with the authority's regulatory influence. A budget manager cannot consider a spending option which may be perceived to contradict an authority's established policy. For example, in the case of the Good Health Board, where it has been decided to favour community care, an individual budget manager cannot behave in a way which is seen to favour longer stays in either residential care or in hospital unless a particular case cannot be resolved in any other way.

As far as individual budget managers are concerned, base-line performance will be assured in their adherence to:

- An authority's financial policies in the exercise of spending regularity and probity arrangements.
- Conformance with the authority's general direction of spending.
- Execution of the budget management function so that activities are constrained within agreed limits.

Size and scope of budget spend

It has already been suggested that budget managers' capacity to manage a budget is influenced by budget size. If a budget is too small, the amount of flexibility is considerably diminished. If it is too large then the principles of delegation have not properly been applied and the span of management makes day-to-day management potentially difficult. It is difficult to prescribe the precise size that can be most effectively managed. What works in one case is often difficult to manager in another.

It is my view that a mixed revenue budget comprising payroll and non-payroll items is best pitched at or about £1m per annum. This means that a unit or trust with an annual revenue spend in the region of £100m would have about 100 budget managers in the total system.

In a mixed revenue budget of £1m it would be expected that the payroll content would be between £700k and £800k (70–80 per cent). Although a payroll budget of around £500,000 would therefore be considered too small to be viable, a budget manager may seek to enhance this by increasing the share of the market. This may be achieved by attracting additional income in payment for services provided to other purchasers.

Generally, evidence of viability is detected in the constant variations experienced by a budget manager. In this particular case, the budget manager has accumulated an overspending of £15k at the end of three months. Where it has been demonstrated that this cannot be contained within the target, or the spending is erratic in nature, then the viability of that particular budget is threatened. On the other hand, the reputation of the manager may be one of consistent performance. In this case the authority may be confident that the budget will be brought into line.

Comparative costs

In earlier chapters, the relationship of a budget to the work-load and average cost was explained. The budget manager's cost performance when compared with external competitors is shown in Table 11.1.

Comparisons	Average cost £(k)
Budget manager	10.57
Competitor 051	6.63
Competitor 052	10.59
Competitor 053	10.18

Table 11.1. The budget manager's cost performance

From this it is apparent that the budget manager is not a high performer when external testing takes place. In a competitive tendering situation, the contract would be awarded to competitor 051 with potential annual savings of around £120,000.

It is preferable that budget managers ensure that their service is competitive. This is achieved by constant market testing. In this particular case the manager should be aware of likely competition and take the initiative to drive down costs so that they are inherently competitive.

Most government departments publish cost comparisons which are general indicators intended to encourage good practice.

Managers therefore need to sharpen their competitive edge so that by the exercise of best practice their budgetary management is improved.

Resource mixes

Most public authority spending is directed towards staffing. Although the competitive tendering initiatives have created an element of competition in this domain, there is still a significant bias and emphasis on the professional elements necessary for a public authority to maintain its services. However, it is important that budget managers ensure that this main element of their expenditure is effectively used.

This means that managers need to review how scarce resources are deployed. It is clearly wasteful for highly paid professional staff time is taken up in performing mundane tasks which could be undertaken by less well paid assistants. In the macro-system we have seen that authorities are determined to alter the way services are provided in order to achieve a better balance. So most budget managers in the micro-system display equal determination to ensure that their internal arrangements achieve the most effective balance.

Work must be distributed so that professional and costly inputs are diminished and menial tasks undertaken by majority lower costed inputs.

Assuming that, the mixture of the range of professional through to unskilled staff is compared as follows:

	Budget manager	**Comparison**
Professional	30	15
Skilled	30	25
Semi-skilled	30	30
Unskilled	10	30

Table 11.2. Comparison of professional and unskilled staff

The preference of the budget manager would favour a movement of the comparative figures. If the general costs were:

	Cost per unit £
Professional	15,000
Skilled	12,000
Semi-skilled	10,000
Unskilled	7,000

The emerging picture would be as shown in Table 11.3.

	1___ original	____1	1____ preference	____1
	mix	cost	mix	cost
Professional	30@£15k	450	15@£15k	225
Skilled	30@£12k	360	25@£12k	300
Semi-skilled	30@£10	300	30@£10k	300
Unskilled	10@£7	70	30@£7k	210
	100	£1,180k		£1,135k
Average costs		£11,800k		£11,350k

Table 11.3. Shift towards unskilled labour

The saving which would arise from this shift would be £450 per staff member, which in a budget comprising of 100 staff would amount to £4,500.

A budget manager would have to bear in mind that the reduction in the establishment of higher paid posts may affect morale and lower performance.

It is important therefore to balance out these factors before any radical movement takes place because savings to be made in this instance may not in the long run be cost effective.

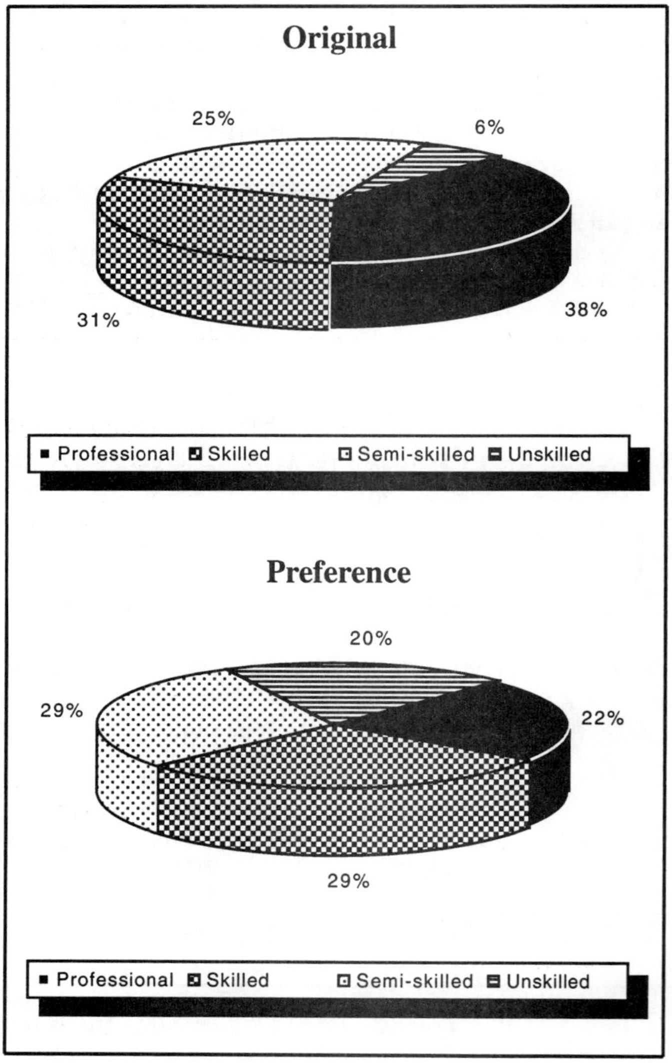

Figure 11.2.

In the spectrum of high-cost options appropriate movement of work-load must be towards low cost.

Budget managers' preference towards low-cost options can be implemented by separation of tasks into basic elements and supplemented by low-level training programmes, thus increasing the capacity of unqualified staff to adequately perform the majority of tasks.

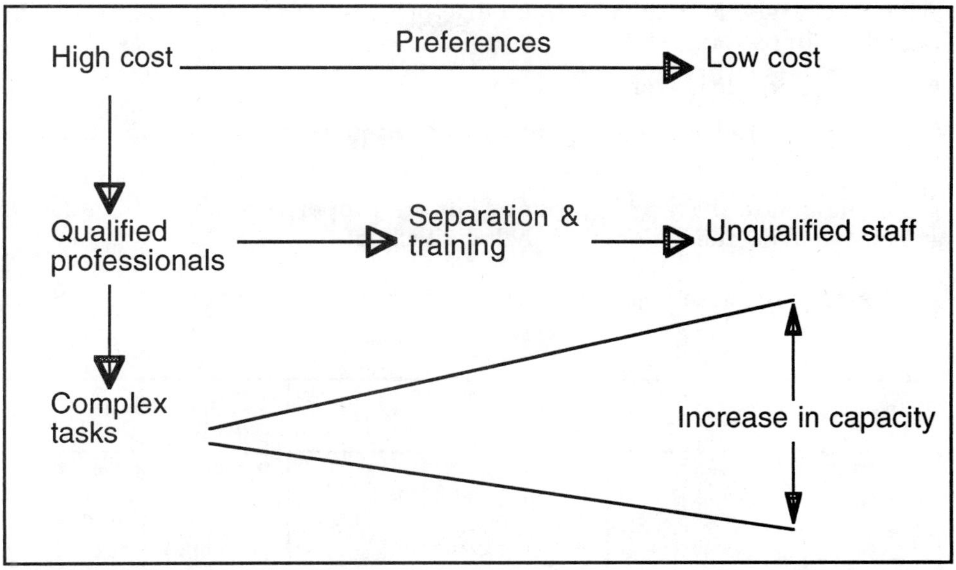

Figure 11.3.

This adds another dimension to performance. The examination of skill mixes can demonstrate further capacity within a particular budget to produce additional savings. In the pie chart below it can be seen that there is a prevalence of high-skilled professional staff. It can also be shown that the range and scope of tasks undertaken can equally well be performed with a lower level of professional input.

Morale

The maintenance of morale is valued as an important contributory factor in performance. Where staff morale is considered to be low, then it seems obvious that levels of achievement will also be low. Budget managers must therefore strive to ensure that morale levels are maintained at high levels. Indicators which are used as guides to morale levels are:

- Difficulties experienced in recruitment.
- Prevalence of sickness.
- Numbers of staff maintained on acting rates.
- Numbers of complaints against staff.
- Numbers of disciplinary proceedings.
- Numbers of staff voicing grievances about pay and conditions of service.
- General performance levels.

Budget managers confronted with some or all of these problems must be seen to take action because they not only impair performance, they may also multiply until capacity to manage is significantly reduced. Managers must therefore be aware of the morale health check and to apply it to their own sphere of influence with the purpose of:

- keeping people in work and at their work;
- maintaining a level of discipline which is administered fairly and reasonably; and
- making sure that hard working staff are properly treated—this does not mean paying them more than their entitlement.

In pursuit of these objectives the morale health can be applied (see Figure 11.4).

In work at work	Discipline	Possible welfare initiatives
Recruitment problems	Reputation for strictness/unfairness • temporary staff • acting grades • disciplinary incidents	• Examine areas for relaxation • Examine conditions and pay • Standardise approach • Rationalise and implement proper staffing structure
Incidence of sickness or absenteeism	Relaxed approach to absenteeism	• Set up a procedure which follows up sickness on an individual basis. • Ensure that staff who claim to be ill are ill. • Take a firm line with other types of absenteeism.
Incidence of • complaints against staff • grievances by staff	Staff discipline not consistently applied	• Examine patterns • Take appropriate action in all cases • Consider whether a policy should be developed

Figure 11.4. Morale health check

In general terms, although it is again difficult to be prescriptive, the following tolerances may be acceptable:

Recruitment— Unless there are specific problems relating to the recruitment of staff in a particular discipline, no vacancy should remain unfilled after a selection.

Sickness— Sickness levels in excess of five per cent should be investigated and followed up with a welfare programme. The exception to this would be where there was an epidemic.

Staff turnover— Turnover rates in excess of ten per cent should be investigated.

Temporary staff— Temporary staffing should be kept below ten per cent unless there are specific given reasons. For example, where a manager was intending to create a greater degree of mobility.

Acting capacity— Acting grades should be kept to a minimum.

Key points summary

- A wide selection of performance measures can be used to maximise budget managers' capacity.
- Managers need to be constantly examining their business plans and to be working systematically through the programme outlined.
- They must include contracting, income, spending and the service they provide.
- A management checklist is given below.

The budget manager's performance checklist

Check:

- **Size and scope of budget** for potential expansion rationalisation.
- **Variations** for significant factors relating to viability.
- **Comparative costs** for potential improvement and for sharpening competitive edge.
- **Resource and skill mixes** for opportunities in better and more cost effective distribution of workloads.
- **Morale**, consistently test state of morale health.

12

Improving budget and business competences

Objectives

Some general managers and chief executives are said to attribute a high priority to sound business and financial management, but management development is sometimes placed at a much lower level. This is often the result of what is thought to be a high cost of development for little visible return. The purpose of this chapter is to show how low-cost, high-performance options may be applied to the development of budget managers in their work-place.

It will also be an aid to managers who work, either directly or indirectly, with the contracting process in both purchaser and provider modes. Specifically will be a:

- guide to managers who are considering improvements to budget contract compliance;
- reference for standards in competence development;
- recommended process of assessment and identification of potential for specific competence development;
- method of dependency on structure, system and the individual for improvement.

The emphasis is on the cost effective use of the work-place as a management college.
It also considers ways in which a more academic approach can be made.

The work-place as a management college

In the market situation, the budget manager must be competent in order to be competitive and to win contracts. This is a fact whether the manager is operating in a monopoly, controlled market conditions or in the open market[1]. In order to demonstrate competence, a manager needs to compliment experience and training with indicators that measure improvement. This is a major problem that stems from the judgement of performance in the work-place.

In acknowledging the importance of induction training and the class-room as premier vehicles for delivering and acquiring management training, skills and education, there is a danger that emphasis on academia might prejudice practitioner culture. Indeed, it is possible to visualise and cite examples of self-defeating management development models, where training and development initiatives were perceived as incompatible with the requirements of the work-place.

Clearly such situations are both counter-productive for the organisation and frustrating for the individual participant: any review would indicate possible disenchantment with the notion of management development and prescribe cessation. However, development initiatives which bind the individual and the work-place in common expression and gratification of need are evidently mutually beneficial.

Modern thinking concludes that while improvement in the organisation and development of the individual are necessary, 'the essential task is the development of the individual in his job'[2]. Business-orientated management development is now embraced in a wide spectrum of propositions and initiatives which cover professional and academic requirements.

The promotion of excellence in management practice through continuous review and modification in the light of experience is an attractive proposition.

While structures and opportunities may change and will change, the basic philosophies inherent in the management of budget contracts are constants. The developmental elements that provide the foundation are:

- The environment, the organisation and its people.
- The customer and his needs.
- Quality service provision.
- Improving business acumen.
- Performance and accountability.
- Accreditation as a tangible expression of participation in and completion of measurable parts of the programme.

In-house characteristics

Work-place or in-house development involves the commitment and participation of local management and effective initiatives are found to be best conducted in multi-disciplinary forums. However, the terminology implies that 'the house' may be anything from a ward, office or department, to a hospital or hospital group. It follows that specific management developmental needs may have to be met at a greater and greater distance from the work-place. While the development continuum extends from the shop-floor to the general manager and beyond, distancing the work-place can be costly, inconvenient and possibly irrelevant to strategy and contractual and operational requirements.

The collective demand of individual managers for skill, learning and research into more sophisticated techniques and qualifications puts pressure on the organisation to create distance and provide time out from the work-place. On the other hand, organisational development and capacity to absorb collectively enhanced intelligence seems to require work environment orientation. This is illustrated in Figure 12.1.

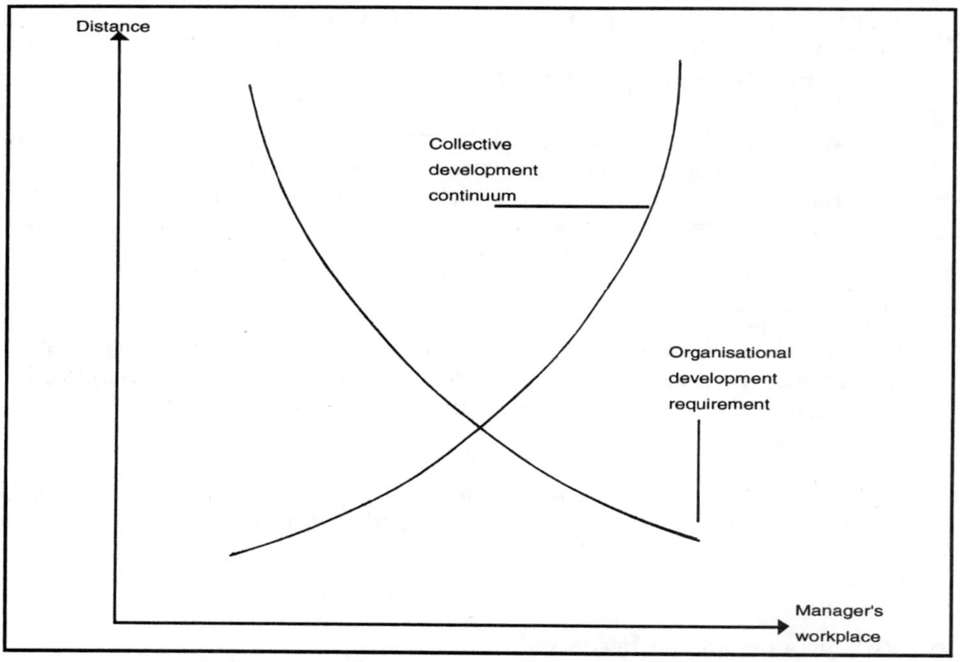

Figure 12.1. Contract and budget competence development

The resolution of this dilemma would seem to require the subordination of the individual manager's needs. This would make sense where the organisation is the paymaster.

Provided that this is not cynically exploited, major management development initiatives should be sited in or about the work-place, but what is it that the workplace has to offer?

The emphasis must be on multi-disciplinary activity. Managers from disparate parts of the organisation are encouraged to identify mutual management problems. Studying, sharing and solving structures are provided to mobilise the critical mass of common experience at convenient times and places.

All managers should be encouraged to express mutual management identity through the acquisition of one of management qualifications, and arrangements should be made in-house through a partnership with appropriate universities[3,4], with a view to:

- Defining the university's role in researching and mobilising competency capability and proposing suitable vehicles for programmed development in accordance with area strategy.
- Establishing academic accreditation for various aspects of work to be undertaken as part of the proposed programme.

- Utilising the university's considerable consultancy resources in proposing and implementing modified organisation and management development models.
- Structuring the attainment of higher management qualifications.

The principles inherent in in-house development are compatible with the concept of the recognition of the work-place as a management college and have been identified as:

- Management and organisational development should be related to strategic and operational policy and objectives.
- Staff development and training are primarily line management responsibilities.
- All training will be devolved to a level commensurate with multi-disciplinary activity, effectiveness and efficiency.
- Existing training resources should be adapted and enhanced to reflect mobility and flexibility.
- Main emphasis and responsibility will be placed upon managers to initiate and implement programmes supported through central coordination, the university and other mechanisms as approved by the director.

With increasing emphasis upon 'in-house', multi-disciplinary development programmes, a number of benefits have been claimed for this type of initiative.

Acceptability criteria

The selection of management development options is inevitably constrained by the shortage of facilitating resources, particularly finance. The wide choice spectrum whose application would doubtless benefit the individual or group described in Chapter 1 must be narrowed to fit the acceptability criteria developed by the operating group. For convenience the relevant diagram is reproduced in Figure 12.2.

The evolution of acceptable measures which relate prospective development initiatives with current performance and need is essential to rational contractual capacity improvement.

It is a process which inevitably must be peculiar to each situation. It cannot therefore be made available in a prescribed manner but must be developed as part of the particular organisational culture.

However, the process should be broken into stages and, as far as competence development is concerned, project management principles applied .

The context

Organisational compatibility in a competitive market situation, is the dominant factor in determining the boundary between the internal and external environments. This is dependent upon a host of variable factors, which connect purchaser and provider, and is finally manifested in some form of contractual arrangement.

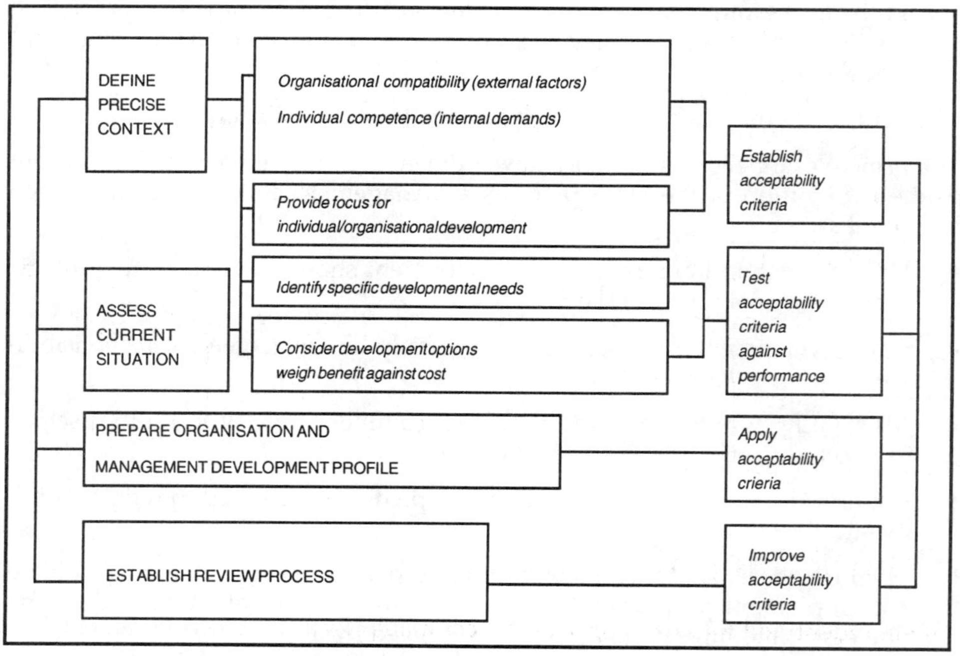

Figure 12.2 Acceptability identity process

Boundaries, which both separate and unify the two parties, are defined in terms of size of the market share. This definition has significant organisational consequences because, on the one hand, it influences purchasing capacity, and, on the other, tends to limit provider capability.

It is, however, most apparent in the amount of consideration which is the basis of business transactions between the two participants. In legal and business terms, consideration is a key dependency when assessing contractual capacity. Inherent in this is customer mediation in relation to income, and the resources which that income will support. Regulation of this relationship must therefore be a prevalent feature throughout the organisation so that commonalty of purpose is achieved.

The management and use of income is reliant on the amenability of the external environment to marketing and on the constantly improved internal environment for its economic distribution. This implies development of management competences commensurate with current and future requirements. Some theorists have argued that the improvement of management practice depends upon the focus of attention on the individual and their context[2].

This approach, which takes account of the environment, was further developed in 'A model of intentions' which appeared in the *Review*[2]. In this paper, Carswell and Cave favoured a more holistic development of *organisation, individual, and the individual in the organisation.* In the same issue of the review, a companion paper[3] described an earlier pilot developmental programme which adopted this context approach to management development and through its review programme, which actively involved senior managers (including the general manager) and participants, provided opportunities for creative organisational and management development.

Essentially the developmental spectrum provided in-house opportunities for large numbers of staff from a wide range of disciplines. The programme design was mainly aimed at the promotion of 'growth from within' and it appeared that the internal needs were broadly in accord with management perception as described in 'Waiting for managing health services'[4]. They are the customer, quality, acumen, performance and accountability. Refining this work, it is found to be perfectly valid in the current climate.

Acceptability criteria can be developed as described above, and applied specifically to contract management, so that a table of competency/compatibility measures relating one feature with another can be drawn (see Table 12.1).

Competences Compatibility	Marketing	Income management	Distribution
Organisation	Customers	Contract value	Resources
Individual	Quality patient care	Budget size	Mobility
Complex (ind/org)	Dependencies/work-load	Budget management	Performance

Table 12.1. Competency/compatability measures

Establishing the condition

Having identified the core competency/compatibility criteria it is possible to test both the individual and the organisational situation so that an improvement profile can be developed. Taking each as unity, it is possible to arrange an outline as shown in Table 12.2.

Value scores						Totals
Customers	1	Contract size	1	Resources	1	3
Quality patient care	1	Budget size	1	Mobility	1	3
Dependencies/work-load	1	Budget management	1	Performance	1	3
Totals	3		3		3	9

Table 12.2. Improvement profile

However, depending upon an individual's position within an organisation, different emphasis will need to be placed on each criterion. For example, suppose there is emphasis on budget management in a particular case, this aspect will have to be reflected in the profile. Where performance is perceived not to measure up to expectation, it is possible to address the deficiency with appropriate cost effective development and to subsequently provide a measure for identifiable learning outcomes (see Table 12.3).

Prospective

1	1	1	3
2	2	4	8
3	7	8	18
6	12	13	29

Actual

1	1	1	3
2	2	2	6
2	3	5	10
5	6	8	19

Variation

0	0	0	0
0	0	-2	-2
-1	-4	-3	-8
-1	-6	-7	-10

Table 12.3. Learning outcomes

From this analysis it appears that the main deficiencies lie in the interface between the individual and the organisation. They concern the general area of budget management but this only indicates potential weakness. It is not definitive in identifying whether improvement is needed in structure, system or in personal development. The promotion of growth from within would therefore be the most cost effective way to secure improvement

Contract and business management

Contract management is an intimate organisational activity which commands the discretion of the collective approach. The clarity and focus with which business is conducted will provide a constant occupation for senior managers. This implies that development must be a priority involvement in the various stages outlined. Experience shows that, in this context, the best outcomes can be obtained through close partnership with management development units and universities, but initiatives must be dedicated to, and clearly connected with the work-place.

In order to meet the challenge of a changing organisation and to prepare junior, middle and senior managers in all disciplines for the future, it is necessary to launch a comprehensive initiative. The evolutionary nature of the initiative is therefore to be continually modified by the balance between the perceived needs of the participants and the ability of the course leaders to deliver.

The main thrust is based upon a determination to produce the best possible package, which is described in the resolution of the tensions created by competing demand. This takes account of the spectrum inherent in the range from the formal to the informal development programme and the equation that relates the capability to deliver to the potential need. Achievement of these outcomes is facilitated through the development of

- An analysis of management deficits.
- An arrangement to make good those deficits.
- Review and modification development provision.
- A manager's life plan.
- A visible career path
- Methods of recognising, crediting and encouraging individuals.
- Facilities for research and project work.

Maintaining the machine

The accommodation of perceived demand at or near the work-place depends on the commitment of senior management resources and upon partnerships with appropriate academic and other providers. As with any other initiative, the principles which govern the allocation and management of resources must apply[5]. However, resource release and mobilisation are closely related to those issues which are discerned as having greater priority on the day. This is especially true at senior management level.

The individual manager-participant must therefore exhibit motivation and mutual support traits which naturally endow the particular development with quality which commands support rather than requiring continual herding and propulsion.

In balancing competing demands for resources, the developmental model tends to foster, and perhaps exploit, these self-motivating elements so that initiative management is viewed as supportive rather than active. This is illustrated in Figure 12.3.

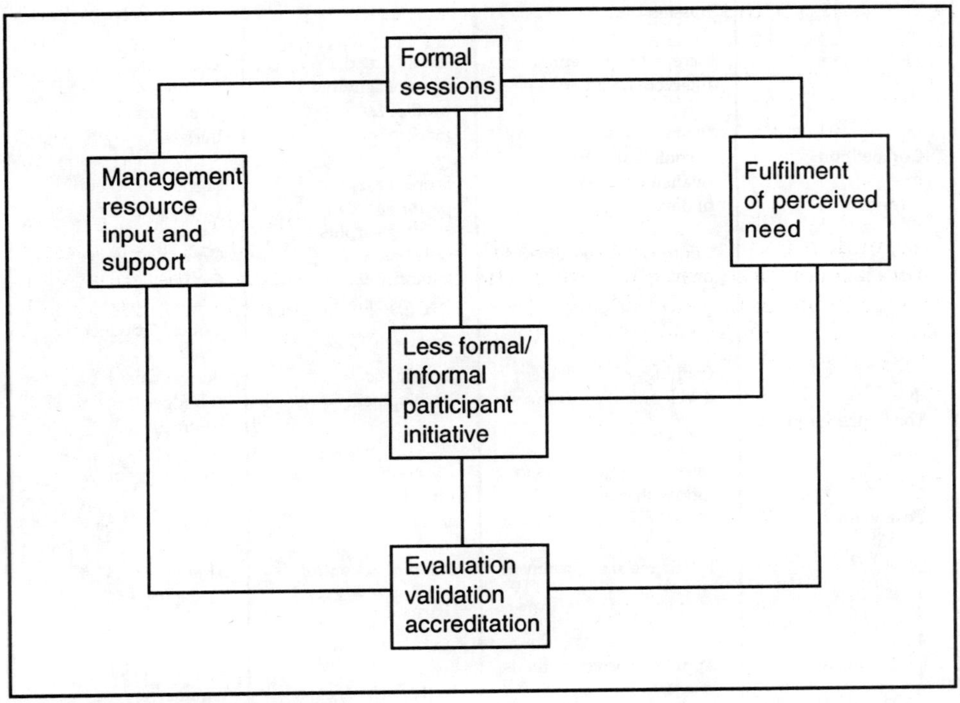

Figure 12.3. Developmental model

Flexibility and adaptability of both the individual manager and the organisational structure are key factors which facilitate this process. It follows, therefore, that programmes which emphasise this dimension must embrace these themes as a central philosophy to future development.

Competences	<------------------- Culture	**Elements** Communication	-------------------> Checking
Audit	Checking compliance with objectives & standards	Applying budget audit techniques	Viability criteria applications
	Organisational & managerial behaviour		
	Attitudes to the internal market	Strengths & weaknesses of systems	Numerical values of variations
	Definition & sense of mission	Flexibility in adapting to mixed economy	Valuing income sources
↑ Performance	Acceptable prevention & intervention criteria	Identifying discrete areas of activity: profiles & marketing	Customer volumes & impact upon budgets
↑ Competition	Planning, quality, control & confidentiality		
↑ Business	Evaluation & refinement of development	Scope for & performance in creating surpluses	Surplus definition & resource mobility
↑ Management	Controlled & coordinated training	Delegation of authority & responsibility	Core calculations & equations relating to costs, values, & budget benefits
↑ The budget product	Training & management development programmes	Systematic development	Budget balances & budget contracts
↑ Cost, value & benefit	Developing managers to cope with change	Effects of turbulence in change	Financial plans & their implementation
	The financial environment	Planning & control factors	Timing & managing a budget
↑ Development	Applying correct methods	Acceptability factors in budgetary management	Basic financial parameters
↑ Direction	Develop business plans	Role & scope of budget manager	
↑ Strategy definition			

Table 12.4.

While the class-room will continue to have a place, the evolutionary nature of management and organisation commands a greater mobility which permits the critical mass of common experience to be more readily shared in other forums.

References

1. Bryans W J (1994) Business Planning for Purchasers and Providers (D.1.4.2. *Information Management in Health Care*).

2. Carswell L A and Cave E D Developments in the NHS: A Model of Intentions, in *Hospital and Health Services Review*, May 1987.

3. Bryans W J Management Development Initiatives . . .', in *Hospital and Health Services Review*, May 1997.

4. Carswell L A and Bryans W J Waiting for Managing Health Services, in *Health Services Management*, April 1990.

Reading list

Bailey D (1994) *NHS Budget Holders Survival Guide*, Longman.
Bowles C (1983) *Marketing Public Transport*, Local Government Policy Making.
Business Planning for Providers of Health Care Services (1993) York Health Economics Consortium, Longman.
Competitive Tendering for Local Authorities: Initial Experiences, London: HMSO.
The Control and Management of Government Expenditure (1987).
Cook H (1992) *Applied Skills in Health Care Management*, Longman.
Donaldson C and Gerard K (1994) *Economics of Health Care Financing: The Visible Hand*, Macmillan.
Efficiency Unit (1988) *Management in Government: The Next Steps*, London: HMSO.
Fielding and Berman (1990) *Surviving in General Management*, Macmillan.
Flinn N and Common R *Contracting for Community Care*, London: Department of Health.
Griffiths R (1988) *Community Care*, London: HMSO.
Harrison AJ (1989) *Control of Public Expenditure 1979–1989*, Newbury, Policy Journals.
Holtham H and Perrin L *Public Sector Accounting and Financial Control*, Van Nostrand Reinhold UK.
Kelehan R and Cole C (1989) *Marketing: Is it really relevant to the NHS?* Health Services Marketing.
Mintzberg H (1983) *Structure in Fives: Designing Effective Organisation*, New Jersey: Prentice Hall.
Pettigrew A (1987) *The Management of Strategic Change*, Oxford: Blackwell.
Young K and Hadley R (1990) *Creating a Responsible Public Service*, Hemel Hempstead: Harvester-Wheatsheaf.

Articles by the author

Commitment techniques re-examined, in *Management Accounting*, March 1979.
Credibility control and the operating margin, in *Management Accounting*, April 1980.
Episodal corruption, in *Management Accounting*, May 1981.
Goodwill as a consideration in budget contracts, in *British Hospital Management*, 1992.
Health care catering management, in *Public Finance and Accountancy*, September 1980.
Limiting factors in budget contracts, in *British Hospital Management*, 1991.
Limiting the financial episode in an organisation, in *Management Accounting*, July/August 1979.
Management development—initiatives in Craigavon and Banbridge, in *The Review*, May 1987.
Non-participating budget holders, in *Management Accounting*, January 1979.
Perceiving the secondary episode, in *Management Accounting*, December 1979.
Timing episodes in the activities of a budget holder, in *Health and Social Services Journal*, March 1979.
Waiting for MESOL, in *Health Services Management*, April 1990.